SOG CHRONICLES

VOLUME ONE

JOHN STRYKER MEYER

Published by SOG Publishing
349 Vista Marazul
Oceanside, California 92057-7343
www.sogchronicles.com

Publisher: John Stryker Meyer

Cover photo courtesy: Gene McCarley

Cover design and interior design by Jacqueline Cook

Back cover photo courtesy: Department of Defense

Names of real persons referred to in this book, may have been changed or modified as a courtesy

ISBN: 978-0-9832567-9-3 (Hardcover)
ISBN: 978-0-9832567-8-6 (paperback)
ISBN: 978-0-9832567-7-9 (eBook)

BISAC Subject Headings:
HIS048000 HISTORY / Asia / Southeast Asia
HIS027180 HISTORY / Military / Special Forces
HIS027070 HISTORY / Military / Vietnam War

Printed and bound in the United States of America

Edition: 10 9 8 7 6 5 4 3 2

DEDICATION

This book is dedicated to the SOG men and their courageous indigenous team members who went across the fence into Laos, Cambodia and North Vietnam during the eight-year secret war and to the brave aviators and crew members from the Army, Air Force, Marine Corps and our fearless allies from the 219th South Vietnamese Air Force's Special Operations Squadron, the legendary "Kingbees" who supported SOG teams on the ground. This book is also for every man in SOG and the aviators who made the ultimate sacrifice far outside the boundaries of the conventional Vietnam War that America saw reported on the nightly news.

ACKNOWLEDGMENTS

After my loving wife of 22 years, Anna Marie Avery Meyer, I would like to thank the following people for their support, encouragement, assistance and roles in getting the first edition of SOG Chronicles Volume 1 printed, first as an e-book and then as a paperback.

Gene McCarley

Jacqueline Cook

Dennis J. Cummings

Larry Groah

Thomas Stump

Bill Beardall

Patrick Owen

Jim Moriarty

Neil Thorne

Craig Schmidt

Denver Minton

Mike Hagen

Lynne M. Black, Jr.

Ernie Jensen

George Eleopoulous

John K. Singlaub

Sammy Hernandez

Alan R. Wise

Robert J. Parks

Jim Shields

M. Lisa Allen

Gary Mike Rose

Faith Meyer Yeung

Joe Driscoll

Don Engebretsen

Mel Swanson

Don Persky

Perry Smith

Ellen Cousins

Morris Adair

Bernie Bright

Dave Young

John "Doc" Padgett

Lou DeSeta

Conrad Bennet "Ben" Baker

David Gordon

Jack Murphy

Cliff Newman

Doug "The Frenchman" Le Tourneau

Robert S. Jones

Ron Ferguson

John E. Peters

CONTENTS

SOG CHRONICLES
VOLUME ONE

JOHN STRYKER MEYER

SOG
PUBLISHING

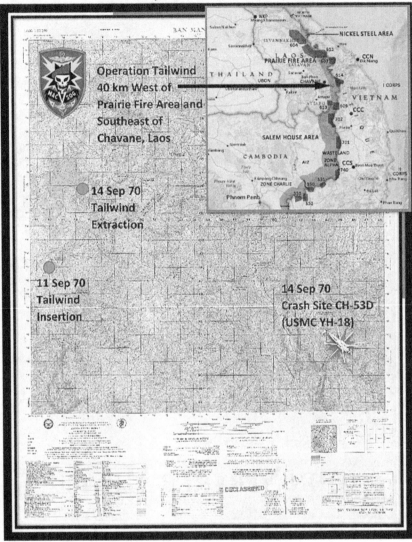

This map insert in the upper right hand corner generally depicts SOG Area of Operations in Laos and Cambodia, west of S. Vietnam during the eight-year secret war. The red arrow points to the area in Laos where the men from Operation Tailwind were inserted west of the routine, deadly SOG Area of Operations, which was one of the major, unique aspects of this operation.
(Courtesy of Neil Thorne)

INTRODUCTION

Welcome to SOG Chronicles Volume One, a book about an unconventional war, written in an unconventional style by a Green Beret who fought in the unconventional war.

For readers unfamiliar with the Vietnam War, there was a deadly, eight-year secret war fought outside the conventional war. It was fought by Green Berets and their indigenous troops in Cambodia, Laos and North Vietnam from 1964 to 1972, run under the aegis of the Military Assistance Command Vietnam – Studies and Observations Group, or simply SOG.

SOG Chronicles Volume One is non-fiction, nitty-gritty stories about the men who fought in the secret war, hidden from Congress, the nation, fellow soldiers in Vietnam and their families. If a SOG Green Beret died in Laos or received a Medal of Honor stemming from mortal combat in Southeast Asia, their families and the nation would be told they died in South Vietnam or received America's highest award for valor in S. Vietnam – not in the actual countries where the combat occurred. SOG men went across the fence in sterile fatigues, with no dog tags, no form of identification, no photos of loved ones or any detailed information that would indicate they were American. Why? Because it was a secret war, our government needed "plausible deniability" if any soldiers were killed or captured by enemy communist forces.

Most SOG soldiers signed federal documents agreeing to never speak about nor write about the secret war for 20 years under the threat of being prosecuted for any violation of that agreement. Photos were forbidden. Because of the top-secret nature of SOG missions, targets and after-action reports were approved and received by key staff at the White House and the Joint Chiefs of Staff. Army, Marine Corps and Air Force personnel who flew missions across the fence into enemy-held countries were also sworn to secrecy, or simply told: "Forget that you went there," meaning Cambodia, Laos or North Vietnam, "say nothing about those missions."

When the secret war ended, the government ordered all records, documents, after-action reports and operational photographs to be destroyed. Among the secrets destroyed was documentation that SOG suffered the highest casualty rate of the war, exceeding 100 percent casualties. How? Some Green Berets, such as Sergeant First Class Robert L. Howard, received eight Purple Hearts for being wounded by enemy soldiers in combat, most in Laos. He received the Medal of Honor for a mission in Laos in 1968.

For approximately 14 years after the secret war ended in 1972, little was written publicly about SOG and its top-secret missions. Soldier of Fortune magazine began running stories about SOG and SOG Team Leader David Maurer released one of, if not the first "fiction" book on SOG in 1986, *The Dying Place*, which was based on his time running reconnaissance missions from the top secret compound in Da Nang, Command and Control North. By calling it fiction, he avoided DoD censures. His team's code name was Recon Team (RT) Louisiana. SOG recon team code names used states, snakes or tools such as RT Idaho, RT Copperhead and RT Plane. Since 1986 there have been some excellent books written about SOG, including a series of 10 *MACV-SOG Team History of a Clandestine Army* books published by Jason Hardy.

That brings us to today, July 4, 2017. There are hundreds of SOG stories that have never been written. In the months and years ahead, SOG Chronicles hopes to print future volumes based on interviews with SOG soldiers, and where possible their indigenous team members and the fearless, courageous aviators who supported SOG missions in Cambodia, Laos and North Vietnam. At this writing, in Laos alone, there are 50 SOG Green Berets among the 1,607 still missing and unaccounted-for Americans from the Vietnam War. In addition, from the approximately 255 American aviators and crew members from the Army, Marine Corps and Air Force still missing and unaccounted-for in Laos alone, about 105 died or went missing in action supporting SOG teams on their top secret missions. That alone reflects the ferocity of the combat between SOG teams and the communist forces supported by Russia, China, Cuba and other eastern bloc countries that campaigned against them fearlessly.

Thus, in SOG Chronicles Volume One, the first six chapters will focus on a SOG mission in September 1970, upon reflection, a suicide mission, where 16 Green Berets led by a savvy, experienced unconventional special operator and 120 indigenous troops took pressure off of a CIA operation deep in Laos and survived four days of nearly constant combat thanks to strong close-air support. It was also unique in that it was one of the few missions in SOG history where participants were approved to take official photos documenting the mission, dubbed "Operation Tailwind." Aviators were given approval to take photos too. Another unique aspect of these first six chapters are interviews from many of the aviators and crew members who supported Operation Tailwind from the air, including: Air Force fast movers, single propeller A-1H Skyraiders, forward air controllers; Marine Corps Cobra gunships, with the radio call sign "Scarface"; Marine Corps heavy-lift CH-53D helicopters; and some Army helicopter support.

Chapter seven is an interesting sidebar to "Operation Tailwind" where 27 years after that mission, Special Forces Medic John "Doc" Padgett met a Russian officer who's father manned anti-aircraft weapons in Laos who tried to shoot down American aircraft in 1970. Chapter eight covers a horrific case of inaccurate reporting by CNN 28 years after the successful Operation Tailwind, in an effort to build ratings upon the backs and reputations of Green Berets and airmen through a fake news story that was instantly refuted and later retracted after Army, Air Force and DoD investigations proved categorically it was factually wrong. Chapter nine, is a Tailwind postscript, with several photos from Tailwind and updates on some of the awards and decorations the men from that mission earned and where survivors of that mission are in 2017.

Throughout all volumes of SOG Chronicles, I hope to have at least one story about a SOG recon team that went missing in action during the secret war, where the Americans are presumed to be killed in action, and remain among the 50 Green Berets still listed as MIA on U.S. records 45 years after the secret war ended. Chapter 10, will detail the fate of RT Intruder from a mission in Laos and an effort to recover the six Americans killed in Laos on that mission – including four heroic Army airmen, and two efforts by SOG veteran, Green Beret Cliff Newman, who returned twice to Southeast Asia in the last decade to work with U.S. government officials in an attempt to locate and return the Americans killed in Laos on that fateful mission in February 1971.

With SOG Chronicles Volume One designed for first-time readers about the secret war, Chapter 11 is about the equipment SOG teams used and carried on missions, as well as stuff that we didn't carry – in comparison to conventional units that fought in the Vietnam War. Chapter 12 is a story about one of secret assets of secret war, Conrad Bennet "Ben" Baker, the man who oversaw supplying SOG and Special Forces troops in Southeast Asia as well as developing and inventing equipment used by them in the field. Baker's success is one of the great, seldom told success stories of the war that merits mention in this book.

Thus, SOG Publishing presents to readers in an unconventional style stories about an unconventional war fought outside the conventional war by unconventional soldiers, American Green Berets and their fearless indigenous troops supported by the best aviation units in the world, men from the U.S. Air Force, Marine Corps and Army's finest pilots and crew members. Included in the air assets that supported SOG teams were the fearless pilots of the South Vietnamese Air Force, particularly pilots from the 219th

Special Operation Squadron which flew SOG missions across the fence during the entire secret war and later for S. Vietnamese special operations units.

To learn more about SOG Publishing and SOG Chronicles, or to reach author John Stryker Meyer, please go the website:
www.sogchronicles.com

PART I

Green Beret Richard Vander Zalnn gives the final pre-mission briefing to Marine Corps pilots in the Officers' Club at CCC prior to Operation Tailwind launching into Laos. The painting on the wall left, is a sketch of SF Maj. Robert Leites, the former CCC commander. (Photo Courtesy of Gene McCarley)

PROLOGUE

Operation Tailwind
A Suicide Mission?

In July 1962, the United States and the communist government in North Vietnam signed a Geneva Accord agreeing to neutrality in Laos, which bordered the northern portion of South Vietnam's western border, as Cambodia bordered the southern portion of Vietnam's western border down to the South China Sea. What went unreported then: in 1959 key communist leaders began working on a series of trails that led from Hanoi and Haiphong Harbor in North Vietnam, through Laos and Cambodia to Vietnam to supply the communist campaign against South Vietnam from Khe Sanh in the north to Saigon in the south to supply the communist campaign against the U.S.-backed government in the south.

That action was formally sanctioned in April 1959 at the 15th Plenum, of the North Vietnamese Communist Party Central Committee. It voted in secret to return to building what would be called the Ho Chi Minh Trail. It was used by the communists during their guerrilla war against France following WW II, until the defeat of French colonist forces at Dien Bien Phu in May 1954.

The 1959 secret vote created a special communist army, the 559th Transportation Group, named after the formal founding of it in May 1959. That secret action and subsequent build up of the Ho Chi Minh Trail was publicly denied for 16 years by the communist leaders in Hanoi and their Viet Cong communist puppets. They publicly lied about their role in the conflict in S. Vietnam, choosing to portray it as a peasant uprising.

To sustain that deception, in the late 50s and early 60s, the communists moving troops and supplies south on the Ho Chi Minh Trail dressed in mostly black pajamas, carrying French weapons as part of North Vietnam's campaign to conquer South Vietnam.

The Military Assistance Command Vietnam – Studies and Observations Group, or simply SOG, was formed in 1964 to take over the lead role of working and monitoring the Ho Chi Minh Trail from the CIA. The communist build-up along the trail and into Cambodia grew in size, complete with troop sanctuaries where 100,000 communists could stage west of S. Vietnam before launching strikes against U.S. bases, Green Beret A Camps along the border, and ally targets. After those attacks, the lying communists retreated back into Laos or Cambodia with impunity to lick their wounds, knowing the U.S. State Department would force the military to comply with the 1962 Geneva Accords. In mind-numbing, diplomatic stupidity, early SOG operations were forbidden from going across the fence into Laos or Cambodia until late 1966. When top-secret approval was finally given, SOG recon teams were flown by helicopters into "Indian Country" to run clandestine missions to determine what the communist forces were doing in "neutral" Laos and Cambodia.

As the early North Vietnamese Army troops and support personnel dressed in black and carried French weapons for "plausible deniability" if killed or captured, SOG recon teams and hatchet forces carried no identification, no dog tags, no letters, no personal effects... nothing to show they were American — abiding by the vexatious, asinine rules of engagement that stifled early intelligence gathering operations by Green Beret-led teams while the communists cranked up their war effort.

By 1968, all pretenses were gone. The North Vietnamese Army (NVA) and the 559th Transportation Group moved more than 220,000 trained communist soldiers south along that trail, along with tons of supplies, trucks, construction equipment, advisors and weapons — including anti-aircraft artillery and heavy machine guns. In addition, the NVA began training specialized sapper units to hunt and kill Green Beret-led reconnaissance teams. At least two recon teams were hit by those sappers in '68, including one attack where three Green Berets were killed on New Year's Eve while the indigenous troops were spared by the communists.

As summer of 1970 evolved, the deadly secret war in Laos raged into its sixth year. The communist NVA and its secret advisors from Russia, China and Cuba continued supplying growing numbers of light and heavy weapons, state-of-the-art anti-aircraft artillery and missiles and vehicles. The communists' campaign against SOG reconnaissance teams resulted in the Green Berets exceeding a 100 percent casualty rate, meaning of the Special Forces soldiers who went across the fence into Laos and Cambodia, all were either killed in action, wounded more than once in combat with enemy forces, or they simply disappeared. (At this writing, July 4, 2017, there are 50 Green Berets listed as missing in action in Laos alone from the secret war, along with 105 aviators who died supporting SOG missions.) SOG Hatchet Force operations of platoon or company-sized missions didn't fare much better.

In an effort to bring a temporary halt to shipping supplies flowing down the Ho Chi Minh Trail, three separate Hatchet Force "Slam Operations" were conducted in Laos west of South Vietnam between March 1969 and February 1970. The Area of Operations was code named Prairie Fire. Again, due to the severe political constraints placed on SOG operations, the Prairie Fire Area of Operations extended west of South Vietnam about 30 miles. No SOG teams went beyond that Area of Operations. The three Slam operations were titled "Nightcap," "Spindown" and "Halfback." Each of those operations had a Hatchet Force company helicoptered to a hilltop on the main segment of the Ho Chi Minh Trail. The troops would dig in, set up ambushes and target NVA trucking. After the lead trucks were hit, there would be traffic back-ups along the jungle trail. Often times, large portions of the Ho Chi Minh Trail were not visible from air, due to clever camouflage efforts by the NVA and their conscripted, forced labor of local indigenous tribe people. Thus, when the first trucks were hit, Hatchet Force radio operators would call in tactical air support to destroy as many enemy trucks and soldiers as possible.

Eventually, after a few days, the NVA massed hundreds of soldiers to hammer the Hatchet Force positions, inflicting serious casualties upon the entrenched troops, forcing their extraction from the Area of Operations. During the last mission, Operation Halfback, an H-34 South Vietnamese Air Force helicopter from the 219th Special Operations Squadron was shot down, killing all passengers aboard the old war bird, including Special Forces medic Sgt. First Class Bill Boyle. Those operations were viewed as successes due to the amount of enemy trucks, supplies and troops destroyed during the intense battles.

The three Slam operations were launched from the top secret SOG base in Kontum, Command and Control Central. The last Slam operation was run by B Company in Hatchet Force command. By the end of August 1970, Green Beret Captain Gene McCarley became the commander of B Company. McCarley was a SOG veteran having run missions during the last few months of 1967 into 1968, when he was assigned to RT (Reconnaissance Team) Florida out of Kontum in 1968. RT Florida ran a series of successful missions, including a trail watch, wiretaps of NVA phone lines and planting Air Force sensors alongside a trail. The sensors monitored human and vehicular traffic and sent electronic reports to Air Force airborne command and control aircraft which flew over the Area of Operations 24 hours a day. McCarley also ran a few Hatchet Force missions. At the end of August, McCarley heard through the grapevine that a major Hatchet Force operation was coming through the chain of command and he volunteered B Company for it. Assuming it might be another Slam operation, McCarley researched the After Action Reports from previous missions. He talked to team members in camp about those operations, their successes, their shortcomings.

In the first days of September 1970, the operations order came down and was assigned to B Company, under the command of McCarley. It was dubbed: Operation Tailwind. And much to McCarley's surprise, Operation Tailwind was targeted for the deepest insertion into Laos ever by a SOG team, 25 to 30 miles west beyond the normal Area of Operations. The operation was designed to take pressure off of a CIA operation on the Bolovens Plateau, which was further southwest and bordered Cambodia. Because of the unique nature of this mission, McCarley drew upon his years of operational experience in Laos for a new and daring tactic: Instead of remaining in a static position like the earlier Slam operations, once the full element B Company, 15 Green Berets and 120 highly-trained Montagnard tribesmen were on the ground in the deepest penetration of enemy territory during the secret war, he would move day and night, supported by air assets from the Air Force, Army and Marine Corps.

It would be an epic mission.

In hindsight 47 years later, although no one said so at the time, most agreed it was a suicide mission.

Taking photos from inside a bunker at Dak To, during a weather hold for Operation Tailwind, Marine Corps aviator Barry Pencek captured a communist mortar round exploding at the moment of impact prior to destroying the Army Cobra gunship. Note the soldier scurrying in the foreground, bent over escaping from the deadly fury of incoming enemy bombardments. (Photo Courtesy of Barry Pencek)

This is the wreckage left of the Cobra gunship that was hit by enemy mortar fire. (Photo Courtesy of Barry Pencek)

Koch, the Montagnard soldier who was the indigenous team member that the only Special Forces medic on the team Gary Mike Rose was training in basic medic skills, gives a final inspection to his gear prior to departing CCC — including packing many extra bandages that were used during Operation Tailwind in Laos. (Photo Courtesy of Gene McCarley)

*SFC Denver Minton waits for Montagnard members of B Company, 2nd Platoon,
to gather after a gear inspection, prior to departing CCC base in Kontum.
(Photo Courtesy of Gene McCarley)*

Montagnard soldiers exit their barracks at the top secret CCC compound in Kontum, which as seen on the sign is the 2nd Platoon of B Company Hatchet Force. (Photo Courtesy of Gene McCarley.)

Gene McCarley and Montagnard medic-in-training, Koch, pause for the camera after a training session at CCC in Kontum. McCarley's weapon here is the 9 mm Carl Gustav M/45 Swedish K submachine gun. (Photo Courtesy of Gene McCarley)

B Company First Sgt. MSG Morris Adair is alone with his thoughts, sitting next to the revetment at Dak To, moments before boarding a helicopter to head deep into Laos. (Photo Courtesy of Gene McCarley)

Sgt. Donald Boudreau, of the 3rd Platoon, stands next to his platoon interpreter moments before boarding the Dimmers to head into Laos on Sept. 11, 1970. (Photo Courtesy of Gene McCarley)

Sgt. David Young, of the 3rd Platoon, moments before boarding the helicopters at Dak To, after the choppers refueled on Sept. 11, 1970.
(Photo Courtesy of Gene McCarley)

A pensive Marine Corps 1st Lt. Barry Pencek stands next to his Scarface Cobra gunship at the Dak To launch site prior to launching on a sortie in support of Operation Tailwind. (Photo Courtesy of Barry Pencek)

Launch time: As troops in the background move toward the Marine Corps CH-53D Sikorsky twin-engine heavy-lift helicopters from HMH-463 on the left, Scarface Cobra gunship pilots and maintenance personnel stand by to launch afterwards. The Cobra gunships delayed their launch time because they could fly faster than the heavy-lift "Dimmers." (Photo Courtesy of Barry Pencek)

Prior to launching into Laos on Sept. 11, 1970, Green Berets and their Montagnard counterparts fill all of their canteens with water before boarding the helicopters at the Dak To launch site. (Photo Courtesy of Barry Pencek)

The SOG soldiers from CCC board the Marine Corps CH-53D prior to launching into Laos. From left: SFC Bernie Bright - with hand raised, a Montagnard soldier, Sgt. Donald Boudreau, another Montagnard, and Sgt. Manuel Orozco, carrying an M-79 grenade launcher and an M-72 Light-Antitank Weapon (LAW). (Photo Courtesy of Gene McCarley)

Montagnard soldier named Bang stands in the CCC compound a few days before Operation Tailwind launched into Laos. Bang epitomized the fearless Montagnards who fought side by side with the Green Berets throughout the war in Vietnam. Bang was the indigenous team company commander of B Company, who worked closely with McCarley daily. Note the scar on his left chest from a previous wound sustained during an earlier SOG mission into Laos.
(Photo Courtesy of Gene McCarley)

Marine aviators provide helicopter support for SOG B Company of CCC.
(Photo Courtesy of Gene McCarley)

SFC Denver Minton leads the men of the 2nd Platoon of B Company from the top
secret MACV-SOG compound in Kontum, S. Vietnam, the top secret Command
and Control Central (CCC) base to the Marine Corps helicopters that will fly
them deep into Laos on the first day of Operation Tailwind, Sept. 11, 1970.
(Photo Courtesy of Gene McCarley)

CHAPTER ONE

CIA Needs SOG Help

One of the most successful operations conducted during the eight-year secret war in Laos during the Vietnam War was conducted south of the Bolovens Plateau in southern Laos 47 years ago. Led by Green Beret Capt. Eugene McCarley, 15 Green Berets and 120 Montagnard mercenaries executed a hair-raising, four-day mission deep inside enemy territory to take the pressure off of a CIA operation on the plateau against the communist North Vietnamese Army (NVA).

Operation Tailwind not only succeeded in diverting NVA assets and hundreds of soldiers from the CIA battlefield, but it netted one of the largest intelligence coups by a Green Beret team in the secret war's history conducted under the aegis of the Military Assistance Command Vietnam — Studies and Observations Group, or simply SOG.

Operation Tailwind went down in the annals of SOG history as one of the most successful operations because of its unique nature and because it was conducted outside the area of routinely authorized SOG operations. This operation went deeper into Laos, further west than any SOG operation in history and it was a success in large part to aggressive leadership of McCarley and the relentless day-and-night air cover provided to the Green Berets by Air Force SPADs, F-4 Phantom jets, C-119K Stingers, C-130E Spectre gunships, forward air controllers, Marine Corps Cobra gunships and heavy transport CH-53D Sikorsky helicopters.

"To be blunt about it," said McCarley in a recent interview, "the CIA operation in the Bolovens Plateau was getting its clock cleaned by the NVA. The CIA came to SOG command asking for a Hatchet Force, company-sized operation south of them to take off the pressure."

The CIA's Operation Gauntlet was launched Sept. 3, 1970 with 5,000 irregular troops with the objective to harass and interdict enemy lines of communication in southern Laos and to clear the eastern rim of the plateau, according to DoD reports.

The main event that led to the CIA seeking SOG help was the overthrow of Cambodian Premier Norodom Sihanouk in 1970 by Lon Nol and Sisowath Sirik Matak. The NVA leaders wanted control of the Bolovens Plateau to improve bringing supplies and manpower into Cambodia to attack South Vietnam targets while remaining west of normal SOG mission boundaries. Routinely, under protocols established early in SOG's secret war, most Laotian SOG operations were limited to 20 kilometers west of Vietnam's borders. Operation Tailwind was booked to go approximately 40 kilometers further west beyond that limitation. To go that deep into Laos required formal approval from the Laotian ambassador and from the U.S. Commander of all forces in Vietnam, General Creighton Abrams.

McCarley, the B Company commanding officer at the top secret SOG compound in Kontum, Command and Control Central (CCC), got the word from S-3 on Sept. 4, 1970. "I remember getting called by S-3 and they told me that we had a special mission. A mission that was deep into Laos, a mission deeper into Laos than ever before and a mission bigger than any ever before in the Prairie Fire (SOG code name for Laos) Area of Operations," said McCarley. "They told me to go heavy on ammo and demo (demolitions). I knew that such a mission would take special clearance up to the ambassador, who was no friend of SOG, and from Abrams, who was no big fan of

Special Forces." In short order, he learned that all of the approvals had been received and signed off.

Later that day, S-3 provided more specific details: Go in heavy, create havoc for the NVA and keep them busy as long as possible. McCarley — a former team leader of SOG Recon Team Florida, where he ran seven successful missions — transferred to the Hatchet Force where Green Berets ran platoon- and company-sized operations across the fence in Laos and Cambodia. "With the Hatchet Force, we were used to going across the fence and getting our ass kicked and then getting saved by TAC Air (U.S. Military Tactical Air support)," he said. "On Operation Halfback (in Laos earlier in the year) we lost Two (South Vietnamese Air Force) H-34s, which included SF Medic Bill Boyle who died in one of those choppers. We got hit hard because we were dug in and the NVA pounded our position.... With Operation Tailwind, once on the ground we were going to keep moving, day and night, to keep the NVA off balance and to keep them from massing a large force against our position."

Although no one said so at the time, at least not outright, the mission that McCarley and the CCC Hatchet Force were gearing up to execute could be called a suicide mission.

As McCarley briefed the B Company platoon leaders, squad leaders, medic Gary Mike Rose, and company First Sergeant Morris Adair in the CCC compound, operations orders were going out to critical support elements that would play crucial roles in Operation Tailwind. First, there was the long distance to the target in Laos: Because it was so far away, neither the older, piston-driven H-34 Sikorsky helicopters of the South Vietnamese Air Force's 219th Special Operations Squadron, nor regular Army Huey slicks could be used to insert and extract the 136-man detachment.

Thus, SOG brass turned to the Marine Corps' aviation wing that flew the largest troop carriers in Vietnam — the powerful, CH-53D Sikorsky twin-engine helicopters in HMH-463, based at the Corps' Marble Mountain Air Facility. Using the bigger, stronger, heavy-lift helicopters made sense because three Sea Stallions, with the designed capacity to hold 55 troops, could take the entire Hatchet

Capt. Eugene McCarley is standing in the back of a CH-53D Marine Corps HMH-463 heavy-lift helicopter in September 1970, moments before launching into Laos on the top secret mission Operation Tailwind. McCarley was the commanding officer of B Company Hatchet Force, based at the secret SOG compound in Kontum, Command and Control Central (CCC). On this mission, B Company had three platoons with a total of 16 Green Berets and 120 highly trained Montagnard indigenous troops.
(Photo Courtesy of Gene McCarley)

Force of 136 men, all of their equipment and extra supplies such as explosives and ammunition, and insert them into the target area.

In previous years, Marine Corps aviators from HMH-463 had performed fearlessly in key SOG operations across the fence and the Marine brass knew that flying combat troops and supplies into Laos always resulted in the helicopters getting hit by enemy gunfire. "In the first day," said McCarley, "it was funny, the Marine brass were a little reluctant to go that deep into Laos because they knew the SOG missions presented extra challenges and dangers to Marine air crews. But, once they heard about the unique aspects of Operation Tailwind, they wanted in."

Marine Sgt. Larry Groah was a door gunner and a structural mechanic in HMH-463 when the operations order came into the command shed in Da Nang. "The most dangerous and the most interesting missions we flew were Mission 72 (SOG support) sorties," Groah said. "We called it 'going over the fence.' For me personally, this is why I joined the Marine Corps, to run special missions against the enemy. I was looking for adventure and wanted to be where the action was."

The Marine aviators were told to prepare for a "Mission 72" insertion deep into Laos. For door gunners like Groah that meant they had to pack extra ammo as well as having a "Stinger" on the rear ramp of CH-53D — a Marine armed with either an M-60 7.62mm machine gun or a Browning .50 caliber heavy machine gun. The Marines slated five CH-53Ds for Operation Tailwind. "We didn't know about all of the hush-hush stuff, we just got our birds ready to go, got our guns cleaned and ready for another Mission 72."

Groah also replaced the .50 caliber machine gun with an M-60 because it gave him more maneuverability and, "if we got shot down, I could carry it and take the fight to the enemy. The 50 was too heavy to carry."

Not far away from HMH-463 at the Marble Mountain Air Facility Marine aviators from HML-367, Scarface, got the op order for Operation Tailwind in a more dramatic fashion, according to Cobra gunship Pilot Joe Driscoll, who was a first lieutenant at the time. "The duty driver came by our room at two or three o'clock in the morning and told us to pack our gear as we'll be gone for five to 10 days on an operation and to be ready at 5 a.m.," Driscoll said. "My first thought was, maybe we're finally going to go into North Vietnam."

Driscoll and fellow pilots flew the early model AH-1G Cobra gunships, with one man sitting in the front seat and a pilot sitting behind him. A relative of the more familiar Huey helicopter, the Cobra gunship had a more narrow profile, designed strictly as a weapons platform. Driscoll's Cobra had two 19-shot 2.75 rocket launchers, two seven-shot rocket pods, one 7.62mm mini-gun that fired 6,000 rounds a minute and a grenade launcher that fired 40mm high-explosive rounds. When the early versions of those Cobras were fully armed and loaded with aviation fuel, the helicopter's skids would drag on the runway for a short distance until the pilots gained enough lift to get the bird airborne. However, once in the air, they brought the fight to the enemy with precise gun runs and rocket runs. Scarface and several other Marine helicopter units had been involved in the secret war in Vietnam for several years, usually supporting recon teams and hatchet forces from FOB 1 at Phu Bai, FOB 3 at Khe Sanh, or FOB 4 at Da Nang.

"When we finally got to Kontum, we had one more dramatically different aspect to our orders: we were told to shoot as many photographs as possible," said Driscoll. Ordinarily, mum was the word. The only photos allowed on top-secret SOG missions were for intelligence gathering and reports taken by team members on the ground. "Obviously, this was going to be different, really different," he said.

In the northern side of Da Nang, at the joint military/civilian airfield Air Force SPAD pilots who flew the single-wing A-1 Skyraiders received their initial op order for Operation Tailwind. The single engine warplane was loved by American groundpounders and feared by communist troops because of the havoc and death they rained down on enemy troops.

Additionally, through the unique design by Ed Heinemann at

Douglas Aircraft Company during World War II, the Skyraider could stay on station over a target longer than any aircraft and it brought bombs, cluster bomb units (CBUs), 2.75 rockets, 20mm cannons and two miniguns to the battlefield. On Nov. 15, 1969, during an Air Force reorganization of Skyraider assets by the 56th Special Operations Wing, 12 Skyraiders, 12 pilots and a maintenance crew headed by M/Sgt Juan Urrutia were sent to Da Nang, based at the huge airfield. The specialized detachment had the non-distinctive title Operation Location Alpha Alpha but had the distinction of saving many SOG recon teams and hatchet forces through deadly close air support throughout the secret war.

One of the key reasons this SPAD unit was successful in providing close air support to ground troops was a major tactic used during gun runs: the pilots stayed close to the jungle, thus lowering the old lumbering A-1s profile for enemy gunners, while providing spot on gun runs. Over the years, several SOG recon and Hatchet Force Green Berets recalled getting showered with shell casings from the A-1 Skyraiders as they flew danger close to the teams they were supporting. Some later reported receiving burns on the back of their necks from hot shell casings that fell from the war bird and landed on the soldiers' necks, burning their skin once they lodged in the collar. However, no one ever complained about those burns — burns that were often life saving.

Lt. Col. Melvin Swanson was the group commander when the Operation Tailwind op order landed on his desk. "To tell the truth, we didn't do anything special when the op order came down. I had no idea where we were going ... we operated like any other SOG mission that we'd supported over the years. We had two A-1s armed and cocked ready to go for SOG missions and SAR (Search And Rescue) missions. We prided ourselves on saving SOG teams. SOG missions were our primary assignment, with SAR as the other priority. When they called, we answered."

Back at CCC in Kontum, McCarley restated the mission to his platoon leaders and squad leaders: Go heavy on ammo, grenades and C-4 plastic explosives, and light on food and water. "I had every

A Marine Corps Cobra gunship assigned to HML-367, Scarface, exits the Marble Mountain Air Facility in Da Nang before heading west into Laos on the first day of the top secret mission Operation Tailwind, Sept. 11, 1970.
(Photo Courtesy of Joe Driscoll)

A Douglas A-1 Skyraider sits "cocked and loaded" at the Da Nang Air Base with a full load of ordnance preparing for Operation Tailwind support. It's carrying napalm, 2.75 rockets, cluster-bomb units, two 7.62mm mini-guns, and two 20mm cannons. This was one of 12 SPADS assigned to the Air Force's Operation Location Alpha Alpha detachment in Da Nang that was part of the 56th Special Operations Wing. (Photo Courtesy of Don Engebretsen)

team member, including our indig troops carry at least one pound of C-4 because we were going to blow up any enemy caches and structures we found, and C-4 is always good for clearing LZs."

Green Beret Medic Gary Mike Rose went through his mental checklist, preparing to carry enough medical supplies and bandages for a company-sized operation. He would make sure that each Green Beret team member carried at least one morphine syrette in a specific pocket. He also made sure that each packed several sizes of bandages and at least one IV. He packed about 15 syrettes of morphine, five syrettes of atropine — he always carried five for insect and snake bites, even in camp — as well as extra bandages, medical tape, rubber tubing, and several NATO surgical kits. Rose worked with his Montagnard medic, Koch, who he described as "a loyal, brave soldier and medic who carried a similar amount of medical supplies that I carried."

And, like many young soldiers, Rose never thought for a minute that he would be wounded during combat.

Thus the stage was set for the launching of Operation Tailwind on Sept. 11, 1970, after several weather delays and rocket attacks at the Dak To launch site north of CCC. It would be a mission where the 16 Green Berets would receive a total of 33 Purple Hearts, for wounds received during the heavy combat that was about to unfold in Laos.

Indigenous troops of Hatchet Force B Company of CCC load up on trucks to be driven to helicopter pad. (Photo Courtesy of Gene McCarley)

Montagnard commandos and their Green Beret platoon and squad leaders prepare to board a Marine Corps helicopter outside of SOG's top-secret compound in Kontum, CCC, shortly before the Marine Corps HMH-463 helicopters would launch them into Operation Tailwind on Sept. 11, 1970. (Photo courtesy of Gene McCarley)

CHAPTER TWO

SOG to CIA's Rescue

SOG Warriors
Take Pressure Off CIA in Laos

After seven days of weather delays, false starts and enemy rocket attacks at the top secret Military Assistance Command Vietnam — Studies and Observations Group (SOG) compound in Kontum and at the Dak To launch site, Green Beret Capt. Eugene McCarley gave the order to move out to 15 Green Berets and 120 Montagnard mercenaries who were based in Kontum, at Command and Control Central (CCC).

McCarley was the commanding officer of the B Company Hatchet Force selected to conduct a mission far beyond the area of routinely authorized SOG operations: This operation planned to go deeper into Laos than any SOG operation in history south of the Bolovens Plateau on Sept. 11, 1970. The CIA's Operation Gauntlet was launched Sept. 3, 1970 with 5,000 irregular troops, according to DoD reports, and the communist North Vietnamese Army was attacking in force, bogging down that operation. Company B's mission was to take pressure off of the CIA's operation by "raising hell in Laos," McCarley told SOFREP recently.

On the morning of Sept. 11, four of the powerful, Marine Corps CH-53D Sikorsky twin-engine helicopters in HMH-463, based at the Corps' Marble Mountain Air Facility landed outside the CCC compound and loaded up the 136-man unit. SOG brass had turned to the Marine Corps' aviation wing that flew the largest troop carriers to reach deep into Laos, 25 kilometers beyond the normal SOG Area of Operations. A fifth CH-53D helicopter followed the flight as the SAR (Search and Rescue) aircraft: in case one of the four choppers got shot down, the SAR aircraft was nearby.

Escorted by six Marine Corps HML-367 Cobra (call sign Scarface) gunships, the helicopters headed north to refuel at Dak To before heading into the target area. After refueling, they flew north, parallel to the border for a while before taking a turn left, heading due west into the target area. As the small air armada churned westward, a small Pathfinder Team was inserted to secure the LZs before the CH-53Ds arrived. B Company First Sgt. Morris Adair, SSG William Scherer, and Sgt. David Young secured the LZ with no enemy response. In short order, the Forward Air Controller, code name Covey, began directing F-4 Phantom jet bombing runs, followed in close order by Air Force A-1 Skyraiders and Scarface gunships.

Air Force Lt. Col. Mel Swanson, the commanding officer for A-1s said the LZ "resembled most SOG LZs: hot. It was another day at the office for our SPADs (A-1s), we prepped the LZ and provided fire power wherever Covey sent us."

"It was a hot zone from the moment we arrived," Scarface Cobra pilot Joe Driscoll said. "We took several hits on the first gun run. During the insertion of the team, Scarface pilot (1st Lt.) Sid Baker and I were surprised by the volume of fire. In fact, we took hits in our rocket pods, we had bullet holes in our tail boom and they shot out our radio. When the Cobras made their final gun run, we followed our SOP, which was to stay in formation and keep an eye out for enemy soldiers firing at us." Because they had no radio contact, Driscoll and Baker simply flew through the pattern to cover the ship in front of them without firing. "The enemy didn't know we had no radios.... I'll tell you one thing that was a hot target," Driscoll said. "We were moving targets, the CH-53s were static targets, but they went in, dropped off the troops and got out of there post haste."

The CH-53Ds were big targets. McCarley said all of the CH-53Ds were hit by enemy ground fire while en route to the target. "I'd never received so much ground fire while flying to a target," he said. "It sounded like a BB gun shooting a tin can," but it wasn't BBs that the troops heard, it was enemy rounds. By the time that B Company exited the helicopters, four Montagnards had been wounded from enemy gunfire. One died while flying back to base with his three wounded comrades-in-arms. Green Beret medic Sgt. Gary Michael Rose added: "It was strange, exiting the chopper, stepping over the WIAs to get on the ground."

Under ordinary SOG mission SOPs, any recon team or Hatchet Force that received enemy ground fire and men wounded in action prior to getting on the ground would cancel the mission insertion.

This was no ordinary mission. Company B moved off the helicopters and was on the ground in Laos shortly after noontime.

One fundamental truism of the Vietnam War as well as the eight-year secret surfaced: the communist forces fought when they wanted to fight. Thus, when McCarley and the remaining 131 members of B Company settled into the woodline they found complete "and utter silence," he said. "It was so strange. The aircraft had pulled back, we were on the ground and there was no enemy soldiers, no noise, no birds, nothing."

McCarley, who was serving his second tour of duty in SOG, wasted no time, the company moved out in a northwest direction. And then the men of B Company had another surprise: after moving less than 400 meters from the LZ, the point element of the company reported seeing huts. The 1st Platoon deployed two squads to search the area. They found an enemy ammo dump, 20 bunkers spread out over 500 meters, hidden under the jungle canopy with vegetation and dark covers.

After setting up perimeter security, the B Company troops pulled together a quick inventory of what they found, picked up samples while demolitions experts SFC Bernard Bright and Specialist Fifth Class Craig Schmidt photographed, identified the weapons and ammo and began setting up explosive charges with 13.5-minute delay fuses in the two larger structures with white phosphorus

Sgt. Gary Mike Rose is sitting in the large CH-53D Marine helicopter flying to the LZ to launch Operation Tailwind. A Marine Corps gunner is sitting behind him while a pensive Capt. Gene McCarley checks his equipment.
(Photo Courtesy of Gene McCarley)

grenades attached to each charge to better mark the exact location for Covey, who would then direct air strikes on that position.

The NVA Phone Rings

While the B Company team worked on this cache, McCarley had one of the most unique moments in his 28 years of military service: As he and a few SF soldiers were looking at a map, a telephone rang. "I couldn't believe it, a phone rang in the middle of Laos," McCarley said. "So, being SF, one of our guys picked up the phone and answered it: 'Hello. Fifth Special Forces Group, may we help you,' or something to that effect. Can you imagine the reaction of the communist on the other end of that phone?! To this day, just thinking about that makes me laugh."

As the SF men chuckled at the phone call, others were compiling an impressive list of enemy weapons contained in the bunkers: 500 140mm rockets; 300 B-40 rockets; 300 82mm rounds; 2,000 23mm anti-aircraft shells; 12,000 round of small arms ammo and 40 bicycles.

Not resting on its laurels, B Company moved north, with the First Platoon breaking point. In a short distance, the First Platoon found a trail, crossed it and were proceeding north when Adair and 2nd Platoon Squad Leader Mike Hagen observed several NVA soldiers on the trail and opened fire on them. An NVA 7.62mm round went through Hagen's gas mask and slammed into his leg. Bernie Bright was slightly wounded, "the round actually parted his hair," said McCarley. "You can't get much closer than that." The NVA fled the area and B Company continued to head north after Medic Gary Mike Rose patched up Hagen's wound. As they marched they heard two large explosions back at the NVA's bunkers. The white phosphorus grenades that Bright and Schmidt attached to the demo charges emitted large plums of white smoke, smoke that Covey readily picked up and proceeded to direct precise follow-up air strikes. Secondary explosions would continue for more than five hours, McCarley said.

B Company then made contact with an NVA company, which lasted for close to an hour, McCarley said. The Hatchet Force men used close air strikes from Scarface Cobras and A-1 Spads and skillful squad tactics against the surprised NVA to drive them off.

As darkness approached, McCarley and the point element began looking for a location to set up an RON (Remain Over Night) for part of the night. "We stopped for a commo check, when they fired one B-40 rocket into our Command Post," McCarley said. Rose added, "we were fortune in one small way: the rocket flew past all of us before striking a bamboo thicket. Thus, when the shrapnel exploded, those of us injured by it didn't get the full, head-on blunt force of metal shards, as the forward momentum of the rocket exploded into the bamboo."

Forty-five years later after that rocket explosion Rose had one lasting mental image from it: "It's funny, I can't remember much about it except that all of a sudden I was flying through the air. At some point while airborne, I looked up and saw blue sky. It was beautiful ... and then I landed."

"Rose showed us what he was made of that day," McCarley said. "He immediately started to go to work on the wounded, because everyone in the CP at that time had varying degrees of wounds. In fact, Rose had a serious foot injury. Somehow, the shrapnel had sliced open his jungle boot and cut into his foot. What did he do? He pulled out an Ace bandage, wrapped it around his foot, used his CAR-15 as a crutch and began treating our wounded."

The most seriously wounded was a South Vietnamese lieutenant. Shrapnel sliced into his right thigh, to the bone, in addition to other shrapnel wounds. "We stopped and licked our wounds, as Rose patched up our people," McCarley said. As Rose worked on the wounded, McCarley established radio contact with one of the two Airborne Command and Control Center's EC-130 aircraft that flew during Operation Tailwind, and regularly provided communication links between SOG teams or Hatchet Forces on the ground with Covey and Tactical Air assets. The day codename for the command airborne command center was Hillsborough while the night EC-130 was Moonbeam.

McCarley's plan was to continue to move at night and if B Company made contact with the enemy, the Special Forces men would determine whether to attack them, or maneuver around them, or simply pull back and call in fixed-wing gunships that could bring deadly fire from the sky upon enemy troops on the ground. By 1970 the original gunships, the C-47 called Puff The Magic Dragon or Spooky, had been replaced by three different gunships, all of which had more weapons, sensors, a forward-looking infrared system and additional weight capacity for more ammo and nightflares: The AC-119G, the old two-engine Flying Boxcar, codenamed Shadow; an AC-119K, which had two J-58 jet engines added for increased speed and lift capacity, codenamed Stinger; and the four-engine, jet-assisted AC-130. They carried four miniguns, two 20mm multi-barrel Gattling cannons plus flares. McCarley, Adair and a few other B Company SF men carried small transistor radio-sized transponders that emitted an electronic signal that the gunship could lock into. Once locked into that electronic signal, the gunships could use it as a point of reference to direct gunfire onto enemy positions.

Finally, Rose rigged two stretchers from rubber ponchos, supported by thick bamboo polls and tied them down with six-foot sections of rope used for Swiss seats (which were normally used in rope extractions from LZs that were too small for helicopters to land). They would now be able to carry the most seriously wounded indigenous troops. When Rose gave McCarley the okay, B Company took the bold step of moving out at night. "I wasn't going to let them tie us down in one position and then hammer us. By us moving, they didn't know exactly where we were. There were skirmishes. A few times we ran into a few NVA. After contact, we'd move on. If there was a larger element, we could pull back and call in a gunship strike. We had flare ships over us every night."

B Company continued to march west, deeper into Laos. The deeper B Company Green Berets and their Montagnards headed west, the more they enhanced their primary goal of being a diversion to the NVA forces attacking the CIA's Operation Catapult.

The going wasn't easy: by dawn, nine of the 16 Americans had been wounded. Rose and his indigenous medic counterpart Koch, worked tirelessly on the wounded all night, even as they moved through the dark jungle.

The only Green Beret medic on the Operation Tailwind Hatchet Force, Gary Mike Rose walks across an open area that the Special Forces men were clearing for an LZ to land a helicopter on day three of the operation in order to medivac the most seriously wounded men of Company B. (Photo Courtesy of Gene McCarley)

A SOG commando from CCC B Company inspects one of the NVA weapons caches they located within the first two hours of Operation Tailwind on Sept. 11, 1970. (Photo Courtesy of Gene McCarley)

U.S. Air Force AC-119G aircraft of the 17th Special Operations Squadron at Nha Trang Air Base, in flight, 29 October 1969.

Third platoon Sgt. Dave Young standing in an LZ during the early phase of Operation Tailwind. His weapon is the Colt CAR-15. Note the gas mask on his left side, which was used during this operation when enemy attacks were relentless. (Photo Courtesy of Gene McCarley)

CHAPTER THREE

Casualties Mount, Chopper Crashes

As Wounded Grows,
SOG Hatchet Force Continues Mission

Capt. Gene McCarley had the men of MACV-SOG (SOG) B Company Hatchet Force moving north well before the sun rose on Day 2 of Operation Tailwind — a mission deep into Laos to take the pressure off of the CIA's Operation Gauntlet in the Bolovens Plateau further west in southern Laos.

"We zig-zagged a lot during that mission because we didn't want the NVA to get a good fix on our position as we knew they'd try to pin us down and attack us in force if that happened," said McCarley.

Within an hour, NVA soldiers hit the First Platoon with automatic weapons fire, B-40 rockets and mortars. Two squads maneuvered against the enemy while McCarley directed air strikes against the enemy positions. The tactics worked. Because of thick jungle they weren't able to get an accurate body count, as McCarley continued to march north. However, SF Medic Gary Mike Rose knew the casualties were climbing among both SF and indigenous troops of B Company.

"We had two Yards killed when Capt. McCarley and I got hit with shrapnel from the B-40. After confirming that they were dead,

I wrapped them up and we carried them with us, as best we could," Rose said. However, after trying to carry them, while tending to the two most seriously injured men, "I had to make a decision to leave the two dead men behind, because I could see that carrying them as we moved, we were causing too much fatigue for the living. So, we made a decision that has bothered me for nearly half a century.... By day two, it seemed as though every day, every hour I kept getting more and more wounded."

At one point, during an attack on B Company by an NVA force of more than 40 enemy soldiers, the two most seriously wounded men that Rose was treating had both of their IV fluid bags shattered and destroyed during a hail of enemy gunfire. "I learned a lesson right there and then," said Rose, "We kept the IVs flowing from low positions, allowing gravity to work, but not high enough for enemy gunfire to destroy."

By that time, Rose and Koch, the Montagnard that Rose was training as a medic, developed a combat rhythm between them. "Today, and even 45 years ago, my mind is and was blurry on the actual combat that occurred during Operation Tailwind. I can tell you there was a lot of it, but when the gunfire escalated, when the NVA attacked us on foot or with B-40s and mortars, or when we moved, Koch gave me danger alerts, he watched my back. He helped me by keeping an eye out for enemy troops while I treated the wounded.... As an SF medic, my attention span extended to the end of my arms, to whom I was treating, unless Koch gave me a danger alert that dealt with the NVA when they were an immediate threat. And then he would help me with the wounded. He would go out and get wounded guys and bring them back to me. He stayed with me throughout the whole mission."

As the Hatchet Force moved north, it was obvious to McCarley that Rose had his hands full as he had to continually monitor the two most seriously wounded men, men who were being carried by him and other team members in stretchers made of bamboo sticks and ponchos. Because there were so many wounded, McCarley directed B Company to find or make an LZ for a medivac to land and take out the wounded. They found a large bomb crater and began preparing the LZ when the enemy initiated two successive contacts with them, firing small arms, B-40 rockets and throwing Chicom grenades. As they worked on establishing a clearing, B Company dealt with the two separate attacks from the NVA, using squad tactics and TAC AIR. Both attacks were neutralized only to have Covey report that the weather had turned bad, prohibiting any rescue attempts for the day.

Without hesitation, B Company moved out again, going west for a while then north, keeping its pattern of movement unpredictable. "What I remember most about Day 2 of Operation Tailwind was the disappointment at having the weather turn bad preventing a much-needed medivac," McCarley said. By that time, Rose had several dozen wounded troops, troops that he had triaged and treated as time allowed. He paid close attention to keeping the two most seriously wounded men alive while treating the lesser wounded.

Meanwhile, back at the Marine Corps' Marble Mountain Air Facility in Da Nang, Marine metallurgists such as Larry Groah — crew chief of one Dimmer — patched up the CH-53Ds from all of the enemy gunfire. "It's true we sometimes used aluminum beer cans to patch up the bullet holes in birds," Groah said. The big, heavy-lift helicopters took more than 50 hits during the Day 1 insertion of B Company. Across the Marine air base, men from Scarface, HML-367 patched up holes in their Cobra gunships.

Nightfall Doesn't End Combat

Night 2 in Laos was similar to Night 1: B Company kept on the move, with continued support from Moonbeam linking the team with Shadow, Stinger and Spectre gunships throughout the night. "During the night, we heard tracked vehicles, we heard trucks," McCarley said. "Night two sounded like a lot of trucks heading south bringing troops and supplies south and some to deal with us. We had our skirmishes that night and we directed air assets to assist us directly and to the areas where we heard motor vehicle activity."

The NVA also inflicted some more casualties in the company.

U.S. Marine Corps Cobra pilots Joe Driscoll, left, and Sid Baker, inspect bullet damage to their Cobra after flying sorties on Sept. 13, 1970, deep into Laos in support of Operation Tailwind. Driscoll and Baker were aviators assigned to the Corps' HML-367 Scarface helicopter company, which flew support missions for several years across the fence in Laos in support of SOG missions during the eight-year secret war in Vietnam. (Photo Courtesy of Joe Driscoll)

By the time McCarley moved out at 4 a.m. for Day 3, Sept. 13, 1970, Rose was tending to more than 30 wounded men: two with deadly, serious wounds that required almost constant attention, fluid rejuvenation, and pain management. By that time, Rose was also running low on bandages, IVs and morphine syrettes. "We were so low on morphine that I reused morphine syrettes, which is a no-no under normal circumstances. But, there was nothing normal about this operation, so I would give two or three of the wounded morphine from the same syrette. I only gave them enough to dull the pain, but allowed them to be somewhat alert."

As Rose focused on the wounded, the First Platoon engaged the enemy as they moved toward a potential LZ for a much-needed medivac while the Third Platoon deployed one squad to maintain contact with another squad of NVA attacking the company's rear. After several gun runs by Scarface and A-1 Skyraiders from Da Nang and Thailand, the rear action force rejoined the company as it pushed ahead into a good LZ site and began clearing some trees with Claymore mines and C-4 plastic explosives.

At noon, after Scarface and SPADs performed gun runs on enemy positions near a small LZ, the first Marine Corps CH-53D approached the LZ. As the large chopper descended into the LZ, the pilot Bill Beardall was concerned that the LZ might not be large enough to land in. As he maneuvered the chopper slowly downward, Rose moved toward the rear tailgate of the CH-53D with his most seriously injured soldier, the South Vietnamese lieutenant with the horrific thigh and hip injury. Inside the chopper SF medics SSG John "Doc" Padgett and Sgt. John Browne moved onto the back tailgate as it was lowered, with Browne supporting Padgett by holding his belt. "I was trying to reach the patient that Mike was lifting toward us and just at that moment in time, the pilot pulled pitch and lifted to the left."

Rose said, "The tail rotor struck a tree and as I was lifting the patient up toward Doc. The chopper lifted upward suddenly. As it was lifting up, it took enemy small arms fire and a B-40 rocket hit it."

Padgett said, "When that B-40 hit us it went through the fuel cell but didn't explode. There was aviation fuel everywhere. How it didn't ignite, I'll never know, but surely God was riding with us."

Beardall, pilot of the CH-53D YH-14, radioed, "May Day! May Day! We're going in," as the CH-53D began losing fuel and its hydraulic fluids. YH-14 crashed without any injuries to the medics or crewmembers, who immediately exited the wounded bird and set up a defensive perimeter, with Padgett overseeing the impromptu team on the ground. As the NCOIC for SOG's CCC Dispensary at Kontum, Padgett could have pulled rank and stayed behind, "But, that wasn't how I did things. I usually took my turn riding on the chase medic ship."

As they set up their perimeter, Scarface Lt. Col. H.E. Newton called CH-53D aircraft number YH-20 piloted by Mark McKenzie, met them at a rally point and led them to the crash site, where Scarface and SPADs made gun runs in preparation for the chase medic aircraft, called SAR by the Marines, to arrive for the downed crew and SF medics.

"While en route to rescue the crew of YH-14," said YH-20 door gunner Larry Groah, "I was admiring the beautiful countryside. And, I couldn't help thinking of all the bad guys down there waiting for us. My M-60 was locked, loaded and ready for action.... As we got closer to the pickup site, I could see that it was surrounded by smoke that was laid down by the Scarface Cobras along with their rockets and 40mms to protect the crew of the downed chopper."

As YH-20 was about to settle into a hover over the downed crew, an NVA .51 caliber anti-aircraft heavy machine gun opened fire on the aircraft's left side. Groah's left-side window was "only about 25 yards away from it" and the muzzle flashes from that gun were huge and the rounds, "seemed to be the size of a basketball." Groah pulled the trigger on his M-60 and held it until the .51 was silenced.

The CH-53D started to "bounce around and I knew that we had taken some bad hits. Sgt. Whitmer was working his gun on the right side as Capt. Cipolla and Sgt. Spalding were at the rear ramp throwing out the (120-foot aluminum) extraction ladder." Meanwhile, Scarface Cobras were making gun runs, SPADs following suit, hitting enemy firing sites. "Everything seemed to slow down as the action heated up," Groah said. "Everything was in slow motion."

When the ladder landed on the ground, Padgett told everyone to climb it and hook on to it. "There was so much confusion and noise, that no one moved to the ladder," he said. "Finally, I said 'Follow me' and up I went. Then they followed suit. Again, we were lucky we had landed in the middle of an NVA fortification. Fortunately, nobody was home."

Groah said the lift off from the LZ wasn't easy and "we had no idea just how bad the battle damage was but we were bouncing all over the sky and we had a huge 'beat,' meaning that there was something terribly wrong with our main rotor blades." Now the crew of YH-20 was concerned about the safety of the aircraft and the men below riding on the extraction ladder.

Lt. McKenzie radioed Scarface commander Lt. Col. Sexton and explained their situation to him. Sexton led his Cobras down to clear an LZ where YH-20 could land. Lt. McKenzie settled the CH-53D down gently, giving the men on the ladder time to unhook and move away from it, before the big bird settled down onto terra firma. Crew Chief Spalding gave the chopper a quick visual inspection before radioing pilots McKenzie and Lt. R. Bustamante giving the OK to fly back to base. An Army helicopter picked up Padgett and the Marine air crew from YH-14 and returned to Kontum.

As to aircraft YH-20, "In hindsight, there was really no way that we or anyone else could known how bad the damage was," said Groah. "Only when we finally made it back did we learn just how bad our damage was." Numerous rounds had cut the hydraulic lines to the tail rotor, one round from the .51 cal. had almost cut the main tail rotor drive shaft in half. That round had hit next to the 'Thomas Coupling' which connects the tail rotor drive shaft sections together. We were extremely lucky to have made it back to base." As Padgett had said, "God was with us that day."

For the men on the ground during the night of Day 3, there was no rest. The NVA intensified its attacks against the men of B Company, throwing an estimated 600-plus hand grenades into the

After a series of firefights with the NVA, men of Hatchet Force B Company take a brief break in the action to plot the next line of march for them. From left: Sgt. Dave Young, B Company commanding officer Capt. Gene McCarley, seated reviewing his map with Sgt. Donald Boudreau. In the background, also checking his maps is B Company First Sgt. Morris Adair. (Photo Courtesy of Gene McCarley.)

defense positions of the Hatchet Force, even as it moved a few times during the night.

By now, the B Company men had gained an important tactical advantage over the NVA. They learned the NVA combat signals during the close-in fighting. The NVA would hit two bamboo sticks together or use a whistle for signals. The Hatchet Force men learned that: one click or whistle signaled the NVA to move; two meant throw hand grenades; three meant withdraw. Hatchet Force men would then radio what the signal was to other team members, so they could adjust accordingly. More than once, when the NVA signaled withdrawal, the Hatchet Force men would then attack when they were vulnerable. It was one more tactical advantage that they used to their advantage against an enemy force that continued to grow on the battlefield despite losing hundreds of men to air strikes, bombing runs and team ground fire.

Meanwhile, back in Da Nang at their air base, the Marines returned to repairing their aircrafts as the warning order came down for Day 4: The weather and NVA hordes were closing in on B Company.

An HMH-463 heavy-lift Marine Corps helicopter, YH-20, heads east with Marine crew members and Green Beret medics SSG John "Doc" Padgett and Sgt. John Browne after a CH-53D had a crash-landed due to enemy gunfire and a B-40 rocket hitting it. A Marine Corps Cobra gunship from HML-367 Scarface is escorting the big chopper. (Photo Courtesy of Joe Driscoll)

CHAPTER FOUR

B Company Pulls Intel Coup

As NVA Hordes Close In,
SOG Pulls An Intel Coup

The morning of Operation Tailwind Day 4 dawned upon B Company Hatchet Force of MACV-SOG (SOG) moving toward an LZ to lift out the more seriously wounded among the remaining 127 men who could still walk. All 16 Green Berets had been wounded at least once, and about 40 Montagnard troops were wounded during the first three days of this secret foray deep into Laos to take pressure off of the CIA's Operation Gauntlet in southern Laos on the Bolovens Plateau further west.

B Company Commanding Officer Capt. Gene McCarley had the point element moving toward an apparent clearing with one thought in mind: Get one Marine Corps heavy-lift CH-53D helicopter in to pick up the wounded and then continue to march, to destroy any NVA fortifications, supplies or troops they encountered. By now the entire 2nd Platoon was being used to help care for and transport the wounded under the tireless leadership of SF Medic Gary Mike Rose — including three wounded who were carried on impromptu stretchers.

On the previous day, when one CH-53D medevac was shot down by enemy gunners, B Company had strong support from the Marine

Corps Cobra gunships of HML-367 (Scarface) in addition to 22 sorties by A-1 Skyraiders; eight sorties by Air Force F-4s from Ubon, Thailand; and Stinger and Spectre gunships working against enemy forces during the night. More than once that night, the transponders failed to provide a commo link to Stinger and Spectre, which meant McCarley had to direct their air strikes from white phosphorous grenade explosions or strobe lights held by B Company men — usually, they'd stick their strobe lights into the barrel of an 40mm M-79 grenade launcher. Instead of inserting a live round into the back of the barrel, the grenadier would crack the barrel open, insert the strobe light into the back side of the barrel, point it skyward toward the circling gunship and turn on the blinking light — which could be easily picked up by the Air Force crew member, who would in turn lock in their computers on that light and then make gun runs based off of that exact location. In 1970, at least two recon teams protected by Spectre at night had rounds brought to within 10 feet of the team's perimeter. That's how accurate Spectre was then.

The men on the ground didn't know about two startling developments: The weather was closing in with a storm front that would prevent TAC AIR from supporting B Company, and Operation Tailwind had rocked the NVA brass into rallying hordes of North Vietnamese and Pathet Lao troops that were moving toward the Highway 165 area near the tiny hamlet of Chavane.

"When we started [Day 4] we hadn't thought about an extraction, except for getting the wounded out," said McCarley. "We took our mission seriously: relieve the pressure on the CIA's operation. Thanks to the TAC AIR we had hurt the enemy, no question, and by continuously moving, we had kept the NVA off balance. We were tired but our morale was good.... We had been on the move about an hour when we heard dogs. These weren't dogs that sounded like the tracker dogs the NVA used on us, they sounded like pet dogs. So we moved toward their sound and the 1st Platoon followed them."

The dogs led B Company to what would become one of the greatest military intelligence coups of the eight-year SOG secret war in Laos.

Before long, enemy troops fired several B-40 rockets at the point element of B Company and then fell back. "It looked like they (the NVA) had gone back to some sort of bunker complex," McCarley said. "After a brief skirmish and brilliantly executed SPAD gun runs, where they used Cluster Bomb Units (CBU) on enemy positions, the 1st Platoon led the assault on those bunkers with a well-coordinated attack while 2nd Platoon covered our left flank and provided rear security. 3rd Platoon protected our right flank … we caught them napping. We hit the outpost when they were cooking breakfast. There were open fires, fires with cooking pots on them. Hell, they never had anyone mess with them before this deep into Laos."

A few NVA hid in a couple of bunkers, whom the Montagnards quickly eliminated with hand grenades. "Those bunkers were nothing but gory blood and guts after the grenade attacks," McCarley said. Again, A-1 Skyraiders delivered CBUs precisely along two key enemy lines, instantly silencing enemy gunfire, hand grenade and rocket attacks. In those CBU runs A-1 Skyraider pilots dropped CBU-25 bombs that consisted of a dispenser unit that held 665 tennis-ball-sized BLU-26 or BLU-36 fragmentation submunitions or bomblets. Once dropped from the Skyraider, the CBU-25 casing broke open in flight and released the individual bomblets that exploded on impact, or they could be set for air-burst or fixed-period delayed detonation. Within a short period of time, more than 70 NVA were killed as B Company swept through the base camp.

As B Company drove the remaining NVA out of the outpost, they discovered a bunker in the base camp that "appeared to be like a basement in a regular house," said McCarley. It was at least 10 feet long and 10 feet wide "with maps on the walls and a foot locker loaded with documents. I emptied my rucksack of everything, except for the extra CAR-15 ammo. By that time, I had used the extra (radio) battery and C-4 that I was carrying and I started packing it with enemy documents, papers, code books, transportation logs."

Within 15 minutes the base camp was overrun. The area was searched for intelligence and photographs were taken as medic Mike Rose continued to treat the wounded men of Company.

U.S. Marine Corps CH-53Ds from HMH-463 (Dimmers) head west toward Laos during Operation Tailwind in Sept. 1970. (Photo Courtesy of Larry Groah)

A fully armed A-1H Douglas Skyraider flying south along the beach in South Vietnam. This single-engine warbird could remain on station for several hours, providing support to troops such as the Green Berets during Operation Tailwind. During day four of the operation, there were several occasions when devastating gun runs and cluster bomb unit sorties by SPADs stopped enemy troops massing to attack the men of B Company. (Photo Courtesy of Joe Driscoll)

By now it was clear to B Company intelligence men that they had stumbled into an NVA battalion base camp that was a major logistical command center and probably the headquarters that controlled the nearby Laotian Highway 165. In addition, McCarley's haul also found more intelligence documents, papers, code books, transportation logs, records, North Vietnamese currency and photographs — including a photo of Ho Chi Minh — the head communist in N. Vietnam until he died in 1968.

Remaining true to his original operation order, McCarley had all of the intelligence documents packed and ordered B Company and all of its walking wounded to march out of the battalion base camp while demolitions experts wired a 120mm mortar, four enemy trucks and more than nine tons of rice for destruction. As usual, after the Special Forces charges exploded, A-1 Skyraiders followed up with gun, napalm and bombing runs to completely destroy all enemy structures and supplies.

Several weeks after Operation Tailwind, MACV-SOG headquarters informed McCarley that the base camp B Company attacked was a crucial station for the NVA's 559th Transportation Group — the first, major NVA group formed by the Hanoi communist political leadership in May 1959. The 559th's mission was to expand the Ho Chi Minh Trail in anticipation of future efforts to overrun the South Vietnamese and American assistance units. Author Richard H. Shultz, Jr., detailed the 559th's formation in 1959 in his book The Secret War Against Hanoi. The 559 Transportation Group oversaw all troop and supply movement along the Ho Chi Minh Trail in addition to maintaining it and expanding the trails that weaved into South Vietnam. Any NVA soldier received a special award and bonus if he captured or killed a SOG operator.

Weather and NVA hordes close in

Meanwhile, back at Kontum, all of the air assets, the A-1 Skyraiders of the Da Nang-based Operating Location Alpha Alpha, Scarface Cobra pilots and HMH-463 CH-53D pilots were getting a detailed briefing on the weather and a sighting by Covey

An unidentified Montagnard of SOG's top secret B Company stands next to enemy caches in an enemy base camp deep inside Laos during Operation Tailwind in Sept., 1970. On the right are several of the enemy structures where SOG demolition experts and A-1 Douglas Skyraiders destroyed more than nine tons of rice, an 81mm mortar, and four trucks before escaping with a large amount of NVA documents, money, maps, and codebooks. (Photo Courtesy of Gene McCarley)

of hundreds, if not more than 1,000 NVA and Pathet Lao troops moving east toward B Company. "During that final briefing it was very clear, today it was do or die," said Scarface pilot Joe Driscoll. "The big thing was the stark seriousness of the moment. Everyone knew they had suffered heavy casualties and now the weather was closing in on them." A-1 Skyraider Pilot Tom Stump added, "The weather was dog shit when we took off…. I wasn't optimistic about getting them out of there."

On the ground in Laos, McCarley pressed forward until he received a "disturbing" radio call from Covey, sometime in the early afternoon of Sept. 14th, Day 4 of Operation Tailwind. "I believe it was Covey Rider Jimmy 'War Daddy' Hart radioed down and told us the NVA were massing and that if we didn't get out of there today, we weren't going to get out period. That got my attention. Frankly, he mentioned the weather issue too, which up to that point in time I wasn't aware of because we were in the jungle."

Realizing they needed an LZ large enough to handle a Marine Corps CH-53D, in light of losing one of the HMH-463 heavy-lift helicopters on a tight LZ the previous day, McCarley moved down a road toward a clearing that was large enough for an LZ. However, the open area was seated too deeply in a valley, which had hills on two sides of it where NVA gunners would be able to have clear fields of fire on the Marine rescue helicopters as well as the supporting TAC AIR assets and Marine Corps "Scarface" Cobra gunships.

To facilitate the continued movement of B Company, A-1 SPADs and Scarface Cobras "gave us fire protection to the front and to the rear," McCarley said. "The NVA kept hitting us with automatic fire and B-40s. The air strikes kept them back far enough so they couldn't do any real damage."

At some point, Covey ran dangerously low on fuel, returned to base and connected SPAD Pilot Tom Stump directly with McCarley about future air strikes shortly before the first CH-53D arrived in the Area of Operations. "I'll never forget it. When I spoke to Gene his voice was as calm as a man at a Sunday church picnic," Stump said. "He had that slow southern draw and calmly said he was getting

Air Force Lt. Col. Mel Swanson, right, was the commanding officer of the Da Nang-based 56th Special Operations Wing, Operating Location Alpha Alpha. Swanson flew close ground-support sorties with fellow SPAD pilots throughout the four-day Operation Tailwind in Laos. Here, he's shaking the hand of Jim Wold, the first OLAA commander. (Photo Courtesy of Don Engebretsen)

his ass kicked down there and all the while, I could hear gunfire down there, explosions from hand grenades.... He said he needed separation between the company and the NVA. We were on station for two hours doing just that, providing close support.... With all of the SF wounded and the large number of casualties they had I couldn't see how we'd get them out."

Providing that sort of support on that day, in that location, with the bad weather closing in while coping with smoke from previous bombing and napalm runs and CBU explosions was extremely challenging. Once Stump and his fellow pilots maneuvered below the low-hanging clouds, they had to be extremely aware of jagged buttes and irregular mountain formations in the area before dropping their ordnance. The CBU ordnance slowed down one faction of NVA that had several hundred men advancing toward B Company.

McCarley and his men were grateful for the close support of Stump, his fellow SPAD pilots, Scarface and TAC AIR, but Stump stood out in his mind. McCarley said, "Tom Stump flew so close to us during some of those gun runs I could tell if he had shaved or not. That's just how close those A-1 Skyraiders flew in support of us. We were extremely grateful for all of the air support, believe me, but seeing Stump was something that stuck with me.... I also think it's safe to say that because this was a SOG mission deep into Laos, none of the air assets got the credit they should have received for the remarkable coverage they provided to us over four days, from the fast movers right down to Scarface and the Coveys."

Scarface commanding officer Lt. Col. Harry Sexton and co-pilot Lt. Pat Owen provided the critical link between B Company and the air assets that were once again rallying around the beleaguered SOG Hatchet Force. When Covey returned to the Area of Operations, Sexton and Owen prepared an action plan to bring in the CH-53Ds to the LZ. For the veteran Scarface pilots, it was simply another deadly SOG mission into Laos.

B Company found a heavily traveled dirt road, only wide enough for foot traffic and headed to a second LZ, one that provided better cover and less exposure to enemy ground fire for the helicopters and

U.S. Marine Corps Lt. Col. Harry Sexton was the commanding officer of the Marines' Cobra gunships that supported Operation Tailwind deep in Laos in September, 1970. The Cobras were assigned to HML-367, radio call sign Scarface, which flew in support of top secret SOG missions during most of the eight-year secret war. (Photo Courtesy of Joe Driscoll)

for the men of B Company. As they moved, Covey Rider Jimmy 'War Daddy' Hart told McCarley he had spotted another "horde of NVA" moving toward B Company.

This time, Hart told B Company to put on their gas masks and directed A-1 sorties flown by Hobo 20 and Firefly 44 based in Thailand to deliver CBU-30 tear gas ordinance on the next "horde of NVA" while B Company found and secured a second LZ for the Marine CH-53Ds to land. This drastic tactic worked. It slowed down another NVA horde, but many of the men in B Company, including McCarley, Rose and others were hit by the gas, which "had a lot of our guys crying and choking on that CS," McCarley said. But, it also bought them some time.

The Scarface Cobras led the CH-53Ds into the LZ with deadly gun runs as Air Force F-4 Phantom jets pounded two enemy mortar pits that were marching 82mm mortar rounds toward the LZ that was large enough for only one CH-53D to land at a time. "We escorted the Dimmers (CH-53Ds) into the LZ. The first run wasn't as bad as the previous day, when I could see dozens of enemy soldiers out in the open firing at us and the choppers," said Scarface Pilot Joe Driscoll. When McCarley lost radio contact with Covey, Scarface Commanding Officer Lt. Col. Harry Sexton and his co-pilot Pat Owen quickly picked up coordinating the air assets with McCarley.

The first heavy-lift helicopter landed on the LZ, picking up the majority of the wounded B Company men, including the three most seriously wounded who were carried in stretchers since being wounded on Night One of the operation. Second Platoon placed the wounded on the first Marine helicopter before it lifted off successfully and headed back to Kontum.

Scarface again led the second Marine Corps CH-53D into the LZ, this time taking an increased volume of enemy ground fire, as aviators pointed out to McCarley another large contingent of NVA moving toward the LZ. Now it appeared that the NVA brass realized that B Company had hit the 559 Transportation's base camp and taken all of its maps, reports, records and money and they directed masses of enemy troops toward B Company. "They told me they could see hundreds of them coming for us," said McCarley.

The second Marine Corps CH-53D picked up the remaining wounded men and several other members of B Company and lifted off of the LZ successfully, drawing more enemy fire than the first heavy-lift helicopter.

Scarface led the third CH-53D into the LZ, taking even more enemy fire than the previously two choppers had encountered. However, for McCarley, Rose, First Sgt. Morris Adair and the remaining men of B Company the drama wasn't over.

CHAPTER FIVE

NVA Hordes, Weather Closes In

For three and a half days the Green Berets and their Montagnard counterparts of B Company Hatchet Force in MACV-SOG (SOG) had successfully accomplished their mission: Take pressure off of the CIA's Operation Gauntlet in southern Laos on the Bolovens Plateau west of their operation while grabbing hundreds of NVA (North Vietnamese Army) reports, maps, code books, currency and other critical pieces of intelligence from an enemy base camp. However, half way through Day 4 of this top-secret foray, Operation Tailwind switched gears from a tactical mission into one of survival.

By midday, on September 14, 1970, B Company received weather reports of a major storm front moving in. Also observations by Forward Air Controllers (code-named Covey) and Marine Corps Cobra pilots from HML-367, call sign Scarface, reported hordes of NVA and communist Pathet Lao troops moving east to confront and eliminate the men of B Company. Those factors changed the operational orders from disrupting the enemy to survival and getting all of the valuable seized NVA intelligence reports back to base and SOG headquarters in Saigon for review by intelligence specialists.

Following Scarface Cobra gunships into the LZ, the first and second Marine Corps CH-53D Sea Stallions extracted the first and

Two Operation Tailwind Marine Corps CH-53Ds heavy-lift helicopters. (Photo Courtesy of Larry Groah)

An Air Force OV-10 Bronco similar to this aircraft served as a forward air controller during Operation Tailwind. (Photo Courtesy of Larry Groah)

second platoons of B Company, which included all of the wounded Montagnards and several of the wounded Green Berets. However, when the third heavy-lift Sikorsky from HMH-463 descended towards the LZ, the volume of enemy light arms fire increased even though A-1 Skyraider pilots Art Bishop and his wingman Don Feld had hammered enemy positions with CBU-30 cluster bombs that contained potent CS gas.

CH-53D Sea Stallion pilot 1st Lt. Don Persky and his co-pilot 1st Lt. Bill Battey were concerned about the amount of rounds hitting the heavy-lift chopper. "On our final approach, we took heavy enemy fire," Persky said. "We knew that this was the last element on the ground and that we had to get them out."

SF Sgt. Mike Hagen said, "I can tell you that big bird was a welcome sight to us. We were all beat, we were all wounded and we all were ready to go home, believe me."

B Company Commander, Capt. Gene McCarley, Hagen, medic Sgt. Rose and First Sgt. Morris Adair held a tight defensive perimeter with a few Montagnards as others beat a hasty, but orderly path into the large Marine warbird as dozens of NVA soldiers surged out of the CS gas clouds toward the LZ. McCarley was on the radio with Covey, "He said 'You have to get out of there now! There's hundreds and hundreds of them coming after you! Now!'"

As McCarley spoke into the PRC-25 handset, a Montagnard team member standing between McCarley and the radio operator was killed by enemy gunfire as he fired his weapon at them. "He got shot in the head," McCarley said. "There was blood all over the place.... Another Yard (Montagnard team member) looked at him and turned to me with a sad look and simply said, 'He's dead.'"

Low On Ammo And Time

A-1 Skyraider pilot Tom Stump vividly remembers those long moments before the men of B Company boarded the CH-53D. "It was a wild scene down there. As we provided close cover to the team on the ground, Air Force F-4s attacked anti-aircraft guns that the NVA had moved into the area," he said. "They (the NVA) really

An unidentified Montagnard tribesman serving with B Company takes a break during the four-day operation. (Photo Courtesy of Gene McCarley)

Three Marine Corps Cobra gunship pilots attached to HML-367 Scarface enjoy a light moment at the Dak To launch site prior to launching for a sortie in support of Operation Tailwind. From left, the three first lieutenants are: Sid Baker, Barry Pencek, and Joe Driscoll. (Photo Courtesy of Barry Pencek)

wanted them. They were massed to get them. They wanted to get back what the team had taken from base camp.... Covey riders told us that NVA 12.7 and 37mm anti-aircraft weapons were opening up on us.

"Meanwhile the Scarface Cobras gunships reacted to enemy gunfire on their aircraft while Gene directed us to enemy troops moving toward them. Keep in mind, we knew all the SF men were wounded and low on ammo.... There was a moment in time when I couldn't see how we'd get them out. It was that intense."

Not everyone was low on ammo. After he was severely wounded in the foot, hand and arm on Day One, Rose had tightly wrapped his torn jungle boot and bleeding foot with an Ace bandage to keep it shut and had used his Colt CAR-15 more as a cane to support his weight than use it as a weapon because he was so busy treating and tending to the more than 60 wounded men of CCC (Command and Control Central) Hatchet Force B Company. His left hand had suffered a shrapnel wound also, which he quickly wrapped before returning to caring for the team wounded. Now, as he, Adair and Hagen moved up the ramp, the semi-mobile medic opened fire on the rapidly approaching NVA after they placed their dead Montagnard soldier on the helicopter.

McCarley was the last man to leave the LZ. "As we were backing up the ramp, they were coming towards us, they were coming at us hard," he said. "I'm guessing the CS gas had them confused, because they were getting too close to us, as me, Mike and Morris stood, but none of them threw a grenade into the chopper. I never understood why they didn't. They were that close. And they kept coming, even as we lifted off" from the LZ while mowing down NVA soldiers.

As the CH-53D, YD-18, lifted off the LZ, pilot Persky said he and co-pilot Battey could feel enemy rounds continuing to hit the aircraft. Adair, McCarley and Rose had just sat down next to SFC Bernie Bright, when someone tapped Rose on the shoulder and pointed to left door gunner, Marine Sgt. Stevens, who was bleeding profusely from a gunshot wound in the neck. Rose said, "He got hit in the neck. There was blood everywhere. I was coated in blood by then, from him and the other wounded.... He was very lucky, the round had missed the carotid artery and the trachea, yet he was going into shock. I rolled him over, got him on all fours and I remember telling him, 'Listen you lucky SOB, if you were going to die, you'd be dead by now.' After that he started to bounce back.... Sometimes as a medic, you have to be harsh with people to break then out of shock.... Then I found something to wrap around his neck to get the bleeding to stop."

First Engine Failure

As Rose struggled with Stevens' bleeding neck injury, neither realized that the Marine door gunner's helmet's open microphone was live. "Communications were almost impossible as he was on a hot mike and all I could hear was his gasping, gurgling," said Persky who was having a potentially deadly loss of power issue with the severely damaged CH-53D Sea Stallion. As the heavily-laden helicopter lifted off from the LZ and went from a hover mode into transitional lift — where the helicopter begins to gain both altitude and speed — engine-failure emergency lights and warning systems screamed alerts of a pending engine failure.

Within seconds, one engine failed.

Persky only had one remaining engine to continue lifting away from the hordes of NVA gathering on and around the LZ shooting at the Sea Stallion and at least one anti-aircraft weapon that was firing at the struggling Sikorsky.

In addition, he and Battey had another major challenge on their horizon: how to avoid the mountains they were approaching, with only one engine. "That ridgeline was sheer granite," Persky said. By now, in the back of the chopper, Rose had pulled off Stevens' helmet, giving Persky and Battey improved communications between them and other air assets as the granite mountain loomed larger by the second. "We were worried as we had to use extra energy from the last engine to get over that ridgeline," Persky said.

After narrowly getting over it, a second granite ridgeline came into view. It too had to be flown over. Now the big warbird was struggling. "There were hydraulic fluids and blood everywhere" inside of the helicopter, Rose said. And, "the tail was lower than it should be. We could tell something was wrong. *Really wrong.* We just didn't know how wrong."

After Rose pulled the bloodied helmet off of Stevens, Persky was able to reestablish commo with the lead Marine Corps HML-367 Scarface Cobra pilot and unit commander Lt. Col. H.E. Sexton. Sexton later reported that "I finally established radio contact with (Persky) and he confirmed that all members (of B Company) were lifted from the LZ…. He further stated that he was operating on one engine. I gave the lead (CH-)53(D) a departure heading and began to close on (Persky) while getting radio checks with all aircraft in the package."

Air Force Lt. Col. Mel Swanson, the officer in charge of all A-1s in the Area of Operations remembered, "This was the biggest SAR (Search Air Rescue) mission I ever worked during my entire tour of duty with the SPADs. We had SPADs, fast-movers, Covey, Scarface Cobras, some Army Cobras and the (Marine) Corps' huge heavy-lift helicopters…. We all worked in concert to get those heroic Green Berets and their tribesmen out of there."

In the back, as Rose continued to treat the bleeding Stevens, he, McCarley, Adair and Hagen were looking out of the rear tailgate where the dominant visual sight was the huge granite face that the CH-53D was slowly climbing over. Skyraider pilot Tom Stump realized it was struggling.

Seconds after barely getting over the second ridgeline, the second CH-53D General Electric T-64-GE-413 turboshaft engine failed.

At that moment, "I can remember (1ˢᵗ) Lieutenant Persky's exact words to this day," said McCarley. "He said: 'May Day! May Day! We've lost all hydraulics! We're going down!' I looked out of the back and all I saw were the granite cliffs. They loomed large. To this day I don't know how he missed them."

Rose echoed that sentiment: "All I saw were those huge granite cliffs…with no engines, I fully expected to crash and

A Marine Corps Cobra from HML-367, radio call sign Scarface, makes a low gun run during Operation Tailwind. (Photo Courtesy of Joe Driscoll)

burn at any moment."

Persky hollered into his radio one more time: "We've lost our second engine! We're going down!"

The fate of the 23,628-pound, 88-foot-long helicopter designed to carry 38 combat troops — but now loaded with 40-plus combat troops and weapons, including all of the intelligence papers, maps, foot locker and North Vietnamese currency seized from the NVA's 559th Transportation Group base camp — hinged on Persky's piloting skills and the six 72-foot-long rotors that were keeping the 15-foot-wide helicopter aloft, biting into the air, descending at a rapid rate but at a rate better than dropping from the sky like a dead quail.

Deafening Silence

As Persky and Battey desperately looked for an LZ, Adair was in the back, amazed that Rose had pulled off another "medic miracle. There's no doubt that without Rose getting to him quickly, that Marine gunner (Stevens) would have died," Adair said. "The way that Marine was bleeding I wouldn't have given you a plugged nickel for his chances to survive.... Then things went from bad to worse."

After he called out a second May Day alert, Persky said he "was hoping a pilot or Covey would say something." After that second engine went out, there was nowhere to go. All we could see was jungle and granite ridgelines. "I really, really expected someone, Covey, Scarface, SPADs or Army Cobras to say, 'Hey! Go left. Go right' Something! But, the radio was dead silent." For Persky and Batty, the silence was deafening. Frustrating.

Now descending in full autorotation, with both engines dead, Persky began following jungle-covered canyons. "I followed one gap," he said. "Then I followed a second gap. It led to a ravine. My biggest concern at that moment was being able to just find a place to autorotate into."

Marine Corps door gunner Larry Groah, who was in the first CH-53D Sea Stallion that pulled out many of the wounded men from B Company earlier, said, "At that time, no one had ever done a full autorotation, with a fully loaded CH-53D, with no power."

Swanson watched the large warbird descend into a canyon. "It was a kind of a depression he headed towards," Swanson said. "It was trailing smoke. It was ugly. Real ugly. I worried that it might explode in mid-air, or worse hit one of those granite mountains or the jungle.... From my seat up in the old trusty A-1 Skyraider, I couldn't see any LZ or any area that was open or large enough for those Marines to land that big bird without crashing. And, by now I had heard they were autorotating, with a chopper full of troops.... It didn't look good."

As Persky descended down towards the jungle-covered canyon, he told Scarface commander Sexton that he was in full autorotation mode. Sexton immediately called the (back-up) SAR (Search And Rescue) CH-53D, as he had the previous day, on Day 3 of Operation Tailwind, when the NVA shot down the large CH-53D Marine Corps Sea Stallion helicopter that was attempting to pick up the most seriously wounded of the 48 men that Rose and his Montagnard medic counterpart Koch had patched up the three previous days.

CHAPTER SIX

All Survive Miraculous Crash

Moments after the last engine in the Marine Corps CH-53D Sea Stallion died, the heavy-lift helicopter was in full autorotation heading toward the Laotian jungle at more than 100 miles per hour carrying the command element, intelligence documents and more than 40 troops — the last elements from the top secret B Company Hatchet Force of MACV-SOG after it completed a rigorous and deadly mission deep into southern Laos to take pressure off of the CIA's Operation Guantlet.

In the afternoon of Sept. 14, 1970, Marine Corps pilot 1st Lt. Don Persky had no time to celebrate climbing over two granite-faced mountains with only one engine in the large warbird. He and co-pilot 1st Lt. Bill Battey were desperately searching for an area to take the large six-rotor helicopter into a clearing, any clearing large enough to land while in autorotation. In the back of the helicopter Green Beret medic Sgt. Mike Rose was working on Marine Corps door gunner Sgt. Stevens' severely bleeding neck wound he received from enemy gunfire.

After the second engine died, Persky descended toward one canyon, which led to another canyon with no clearing in sight. "To be blunt, there was no fucking place to go," Persky said.

And then divine intervention: Persky and Battey saw a body of water, "with a little patch of beach. It was just blind luck. We didn't know what was there, or, God was with us," Persky said. With blood, hydraulic fluid and aviation fuel leaking and pooling in the passenger compartment, Persky headed in that direction.

At first, he thought about landing in the water, to buffer some of the impact of landing. "Then I remembered," Persky said, "we had wounded in the back. I didn't want to take a chance of having anyone drowning." So he headed the wounded chopper toward what appeared to be a sandy beach area next to the water, even though it was slanted to the right.

All of this happened in a matter of seconds.

"We were going down about 6,000 feet a minute," he said. "At that point we needed high air speed to use the energy to keep the rotors going" so the autorotation factor would keep the aircraft moving forward, instead of dropping from the sky. The plan was to flare, a procedure where the rotors' angle of pitch is changed to slow down the rate of descent and minimize the severity of impact upon landing on terra firma.

"I started to flare, thinking we had enough time to decrease our speed more.... I pulled the collective hard. I had it pulled up to my armpit." In a helicopter the collective lever is on the left side of the pilot's seat, and it changes the pitch angle on the helicopter's main rotors. In this case Persky was decreasing the Sea Stallion's speed, hoping to minimize the final impact of landing in full autoration — something no aviator had done up to that point in time with a loaded helicopter. Persky added, "It didn't slow our air speed as much as I had hoped it would. It was supposed to cushion us more. It didn't." What's more, that beach had a huge boulder on it that slanted to the right.

Violent Impact — Teeth Crumble

The 23,628-pound helicopter violently landed on the angled slope, hitting the sloped surface and instantly slamming to the right, into the ground, ejecting several of the Green Berets and their Montagnard tribesmen team members while the six rotors shattered upon impact with the ground.

B Company commanding officer Capt. Gene McCarley, was violently slammed into the roof of the helicopter, before being ejected from it. "I remember hitting the roof of the helicopter. I remember hitting it so hard I felt my teeth crumble into sand," McCarley said 45 years later.

"The next thing I knew, I was outside on a rock…. We were all dazed. Amazed we were still alive."

Rose said, "When you pancake in like we did on a helicopter and when it hits violently upside down, everybody had their bell rung. Trust me we were all hurting. Gene was bleeding from the mouth, but he could move. I remember getting thrown out and the blades were upside down. I was bleary-eyed, still not getting all of my senses back, and for a moment I thought the chopper was coming toward me."

McCarley said, "Mike was standing beside me, I was wiping the blood and my crushed teeth from my mouth. Then Mike said, 'We've got people in there. We have to get them out.' I could smell the aviation fuel, there was blood everywhere, there was hydraulic fluids, the helicopter was broken by the severity of the crash and it was smoking. How it didn't explode, I'll never know. How that young Marine pilot landed, albeit a hard landing, I'll never know."

Then McCarley had one of those unique, inexplicable moments in wartime: In the middle of all the rubble, the smoke, the dazed confusion at the crash site, he looked to his right and observed First Sgt. Morris Adair standing in water with a smile on his face, holding his CAR-15.

It seemed surreal because:
- After four days of intense combat that killed three Montagnard team members and wounded all 16 Green Berets — some more than once, during fighting in the jungles of Laos;
- After barely escaping from the LZ on the last helicopter a few minutes earlier with hordes of commu-

nist North Vietnamese Army (NVA) soldiers rushing
the aircraft;
- After having double engine failure and losing all
power over the mountains of Laos;
- And after surviving a crash landing deep inside Laos,
there was a smiling Adair standing in the water.

"That scene was unreal beyond description," McCarley said.
"Of all the times that I had been in Laos I had never seen a scene
like this: A body of water, a nice white sandy beach. It looked just
like Hawaii. And there's Adair standing in the water as though there
wasn't a care in the world."

"To this day, I can't explain what exactly happened that day,"
Adair said. "I came out on my own, but I've been trying to figure
out how ever since. When I came to my senses, I was standing in
the water. Gene later told me I was standing there smiling. Can't
tell you why I was smiling, maybe I was just happy to still be alive
after getting my bell rung.... We were batted around like BBs in that
chopper when it crashed.... At the time, I didn't realize how much
damage had been done to my nerves on the left side of my body, my
head, neck, shoulder, arms and hip."

Back To Reality

The brief reverie ended when Rose and McCarley headed back
into the smoking helicopter.

"Rose helped to carry out (SF 1st Lt.) Pete Landon, who had only
been in country one week when Operation Tailwind launched," Mc-
Carley said. Landon, the platoon leader had a bad gash on his head
that Rose had to tend to as there was a lot of blood flowing from the
head wound. McCarley gathered the intelligence materials B Company had collected. "That was the first thing I did: recover the intel
documents, maps, currency, etc. that we had seized from that NVA
base camp. No way were we going back to Kontum without them."

After setting up a hasty perimeter at the rear of the broken Sikorsky
helicopter, McCarley returned to help SFC Bernie Bright get untan-

gled from wires and debris inside the aircraft. Then they exited the helicopter to strengthen the perimeter around the backside of it.

In the pilots' compartment, Persky unstrapped Battey who had a bad back compression, stemming from the crash. "I kinda pulled Bill from the helicopter. He was mobile, but still stunned."

When Persky set Battey down on the ground in front of the helicopter, he didn't see any SF men on that side of the bird. "My infantryman tactics kicked in. We circled the wagons, set up a rough perimeter" in front of the Sea Stallion, Persky said.

In the back of the helicopter, Rose, McCarley and Mike Hagen helped the stunned troops to exit the helicopter. "Before I'd let any of the injured get off of the helicopter, I draped their weapons, or any weapon near them, around their neck so that when they set up in the perimeter, they'd be able to defend themselves," said Rose.

By that point in time, "We were strictly working on adrenaline," he added. "It's funny how the mind works," he added. "On Day Three, I started to feel tired and felt the pain in my foot (from the hot metal shrapnel wound that cut through his jungle boot and into his foot on Day One) even when I saw the [Marine CH-53D] helicopter coming in to pick up our wounded, I could feel the fatigue. However, when that chopper got shot down, the adrenaline kicked in again on Day Three.... The same thing happened on Day Four: I started to feel tired, my foot started registering pain in my mind. Then we got shot down. Then, we were working on adrenaline, helping to get everyone off of the smoking bird."

A-1 Skyraider pilot Lt. Tom Stump, who remained over the target area, said, "They went down hard. Real hard. I was amazed that the pilot found that boulder to land on and that people survived that crash."

As soon as the A-1 Skyraider pilots determined that there were survivors at the crash site in the canyon valley, "We set up a weave pattern, using four A-1s around that downed chopper," said Air Force Lt. Col. Mel Swanson, the squadron leader of the Skyraiders based in Da Nang and Thailand. "Believe me, we stayed low and slow to figure out the best approach for the (rescue) chopper."

Moments after exiting the Marines Corps CH-53D helicopter in the background following the extraction from Laos, Sp.5 Craig Schmidt, center, holds a portrait of North Vietnam's venerated communist leader Ho Chi Minh that was seized when B Company overran an enemy base camp deep inside Laos. On the left is Sgt. Manuel Orazco, with Sgt. Donald Boudreau on the right. The battle-weary Green Beret trio is standing on the helipad at CCC Kontum.
(Photo Courtesy of Gene McCarley)

Recouping, Regrouping

As the remaining dazed and wounded Green Berets and their Montagnard B Company counterparts gathered their collective wits, strengthened their perimeter at the rear of the CH-53D and consolidated whatever ammo was left, Lt. Col. H. E. Sexton, the lead Marine Corps HML-367 Scarface Cobra pilot and unit commander made radio contact with the backup Marine Corps HMH-463 CH-53D co-piloted by Lt. J. Tucker and Lt. R. Arnold and gave them a vector to the crash site.

Once again time was working against the men on the ground.

"I forget how long it took from the time that we crashed until I received radio contact either from [Lt.] Col. Sexton or Covey (the Forward Air Controller)," said McCarley. They told him that the back-up helicopter's fuel levels were getting low and that when he came into the LZ, we'd only have five minutes or less to get the hell out of there or we might not have enough aviation fuel to make it back to Dak To," the launch and refueling site for SOG missions run out of CCC in Kontum.

After dodging Russian-assisted NVA anti-aircraft weapons, including Russian-manufactured ack-ack weapons that exploded in mid-air in the fashion of anti-aircraft weapons of World War II, and hundreds of enemy ground forces firing automatic weapons and Rocket-Propelled Grenades at them, pilots in the first Scarface Cobras that led the rescue helicopter toward the LZ were surprised to receive no enemy ground fire.

The heavy-lift Marine Sea Stallion followed closely behind the Scarface gunships. Due to the heavy enemy ground fire throughout Operation Tailwind, to provide extra defensive firepower for the big helicopter, Capt. H. Cipolla was on the rear ramp with an M-60 machine gun, in addition to right door gunner SSG T. McBride and left door gunner Sgt. T. Winnicki, and Crew Chief Sgt. Smith

Maggots Help Medics

"Even though we had our bell rung, when that chase ship (back-

Green Beret medic Gary Mike Rose, center leaves the helipad at CCC Kontum with a cold can of beer, escorted by SSG Sturgeon, left, and Charles Thomas, right. Rose was wounded twice on the first day of the mission — to this day, he has limited movement in his left hand due to the serious nerve and muscle damage he sustained on day one of the operation from shrapnel. As the only Special Forces medic on Operation Tailwind, he was busy tending to the wounded throughout the four-day mission. (Photo Courtesy of Gene McCarley)

up helicopter) landed, we didn't waste time getting aboard it," said Rose. "I remember Mike (Hagen), Gene, and First Sergeant (Adair) helping people up the ramp."

Marine Pilot Persky knew that he had bitten through his lip upon crash impact, but he didn't realize how severely damaged it was until he moved up the ramp of the CH-53D and one of the door gunners pointed out that his lower lip was merely hanging by a thin piece of skin. "He told me that I better hold on to my lip or I'd likely lose it…I do remember they changed my call sign afterwards to 'Lip'."

As the Sea Stallion lifted off with the wounded and extremely fatigued men of B Company, Rose made another surprising discovery: Maggots had helped to treat the two most seriously wounded team members who had been carried since the command post was struck by an RPG round during Day One. When that RPG hit, Rose had suffered serious wounds in two places, McCarley in several places and two indigenous team members had been seriously incapacitated.

"The one thing that I never thought about or planned for," said Rose, "was for the use of maggots, which in the end proved to be the most likely life saver for the two most-critically wounded team members." During those four days on the ground, Rose and the Montagnard medic trainee Koch, were kept busy caring for them, giving them extra fluids, morphine shots and IVs. But, during those days, "flies laid their eggs in the wounds of the most seriously injured and a few other Yards (Montagnards) and they hatched," Rose said. "According to the doctors at the evacuation hospital, the maggots got to the necrotic flesh before infection could set in and in fact did a better job debriding the wounds than a surgeon could do. Who would have thought of it?"

The CH-53D returned to Dak To to refuel while A-1 pilots Swanson and Stump destroyed the crashed CH-53D. The rescue Sea Stallion then returned B Company to the LZ outside the top secret SOG compound in Kontum, Command and Control Central (CCC). An S-2 officer approached McCarley and took his rucksack, which contained the enemy currency and some of the intelligence docu-

This is a classic example of just how close to the treetops pilots flew the single-propeller A-1H Skyraiders when making gun runs over a target. Here, the contrails are left behind by the low-flying Skyraider. Green Berets on the ground during Operation Tailwind said the tactical support from Skyraiders and other air support resulted in hundreds of enemy soldiers killed. (Photo Courtesy of Don Fulton)

ments collected from the NVA command post in Laos. "I never saw that rucksack nor the NVA currency again," McCarley lamented.

"Regardless, the mission was dubbed a success by the folks in Saigon and at SOG Headquarters. We were told that thanks to our efforts, the CIA's Operation Gauntlet was able to regain control of the strong point atop the Bolovens Plateau 10 days after we were extracted on the final helicopter. We had tied down an estimated regiment of NVA and Pathet Lao forces while destroying one major enemy ammo dump and an enemy base camp after we removed the enemy documents and maps."

A subsequent DoD report confirmed McCarley's final analysis that Operation Tailwind was SOG's deepest penetration into Laos during the eight-year secret war.

The final count: Three Montagnards were killed in action, 33 were listed as wounded in action. A total of 33 Purple Hearts were awarded to the 16 Green Berets who served on Operation Tailwind for wounds they received during the four-day mission. McCarley required nine months of dental repair and surgery due to crushing his teeth when the CH-53D crashed.

Two days after the Green Berets returned to CCC, completed their reports and got patched up by Special Forces medics on base, a huge party was held in Kontum base, with food, soda and alcohol for all of the participants in Operation Tailwind, including the aviators from the Dimmers HMH-463 unit, Scarface Cobra gun ship crews, Army Cobra gun ship crews and some Air Force Covey pilots. Somehow the word didn't get delivered to the A-1 SPAD pilots and ground crews from the Da Nang based OLAA command. Forty-seven years later, Swanson mused, "It's just as good that we didn't get the word, because we were busy supporting other SOG and SAR missions. You know, just another day in the Prairie Fire Area of Operations for our Skyraiders."

To this day, Rose can't touch the thumb on his left hand with his little finger due to the serious nerve and muscle damage he received when wounded on Day One. For more than two years, his wife pulled puss-coated shrapnel and bamboo shards from his body

The Montagnard tribesman named Koch is all smiles moments after exiting the last Marine Corps heavy-lift CH-53D Sea Stallion Sikorsky helicopter. SF Medic Mike Rose was in the process of training Koch in fundamental medic skills before and during the mission. He was one of the 49 men from B Company CCC who were wounded during the mission. Of the 136 men who left Kontum on Sept. 11, 1970, three Montagnard team members were killed in action and three were wounded en route to the target. (Photo Courtesy of Gene McCarley).

stemming from the many times he was hit with enemy shrapnel while on the ground.

Adair still suffers from nerve damage to his neck, left shoulder and left arm from Operation Tailwind.

28 years later, CNN broadcast a factually inaccurate story that misreported Operation Tailwind, while — in the opinions of the brave men who fought in it — attacking their integrity and the true success of that historic SOG mission.

Moments after the Marine Corps Dimmer landed at CCC in Kontum, Tailwind team members exited the chopper and were greeted by fellow officers and troops, from left: 1st Platoon Sgt. Manuel Orozco, Lt. Col Scalize — the CCC acting commander, with no hat and back turned to camera, Sgt. Maker — who didn't go on the mission and, Major Vic Gilliland — on the right, with his back to the camera. (Photo Courtesy of Gene McCarley)

Marine Corps pilot Lt. Joe Driscoll inspects bullet holes in his Cobra gunship received while supporting the B Company Hatchet Force during Operation Tailwind in Laos. (Photo Courtesy of Joe Driscoll)

An American Colt CAR-15 sits on top of a box of enemy mortar rounds discovered in an enemy cache during Operation Tailwind. It was destroyed in Laos by the Hatchet Force. (Photo Courtesy of Gene McCarley)

Marine Corps HML-367 Cobra gunship pilot 1st Lt. Barry Pencek, call sign Scarface 20, stands next to his Cobra pointing to a bullet hole in that helicopter's drive shaft from enemy gunfire. Fortunately, the gunship was able to return to Dak To, where ground crew staff repaired the warbird. (Photo Courtesy of Barry Pencek)

A rare photograph taken on the ground in Laos on Day three of Operation Tailwind, as Green Berets clear an LZ for a Marine Corps CH-53D helicopter to land and pick up the most seriously wounded men. The LZ later became a hot bed of enemy activity as communist soldiers shot down one of the twin-engine heavy-lift helicopters that day. This photo shows how high and dense jungle vegetation can grow in Southeast Asia. (Photo Courtesy of Gene McCarley)

SPAD pilot 1st Lt. Tom Stump standing next to an A-1H Skyraider prior to launching on a Prairie Fire Mission in Laos. (Photo Courtesy of Tom Stump)

Air Force 1st Lt. Tom Stump standing in front of an A-1H Skyraider, in Da Nang, fully armed and ready to launch on a mission. (Photo Courtesy of Tom Stump)

SFC Bernie Bright is welcomed back to CCC in Kontum after returning from Operation Tailwind. (Photo Courtesy of Gene McCarley)

Fatigue is etched upon the face of 1st Sgt., MSG Morris Adair upon his return from Operation Tailwind on Sept. 14, 1970. (Photo Courtesy of Gene McCarley)

S.F. Medic John "Doc" Padgett posing for a rare photo op with fellow members of Special Forces A Camp Bong Son, A-227 in South Vietnam. Doc is kneeling, second from left in the front row. (Photo Courtesy of John "Doc" Padgett)

CHAPTER SEVEN

"Doc" Learns Tailwind–Russia Link

Twenty-seven years after Green Beret medic John "Doc" Padgett survived the crash of the CH-53D helicopter during the third day of Operation Tailwind, he had what can best be termed as a "small-world" incident which related to the Sept. 13, 1970 crash in Laos.

In 1997 Padgett was a member of a detachment from the 46th Civil Affairs Battalion, USAR, which was as deployed to Kazakhstan to develop contacts and relations with the Kazakh armed forces. The reasoning behind sending the detachment to Kazakhstan on a humanitarian mission? It would be the best way to launch an initial contact between the two forces. The small detachment sent to the ninth largest country in the world consisted of Padgett — a PA, an orthopedic surgeon, a dentist, medics and a few admin-support types.

This was a historic first visit for U.S. troops to this central Asia country since the break up of the Soviet Union six years earlier, in 1991. Kazakhstan was bordered by the Russia to the north, China to the east and Kyrgyzstan, Uzbekistan, Turkmenistan and the Caspian Sea to the south and west. The Kazakhstan army was composed of mostly ethnic Russians whose families had long since settled there in a country where there were 131 ethnicities, including Kazakhs, who

Here's a classic example of what the well dressed Special Operations officer, complete with stylish accessories, wears while preparing to motor stately through Baghdad while serving in Central Asia. Padgett was a Civil Affairs Public Health Team leader in Baghdad 2003-04. (Photo Courtesy of John E. "Doc" Padgett)

consisted of 63 percent of the population. Kazakhstan was to Russia what the west was to the United States: open spaces with nomads and lots of land. It was settled in much the same way. The Kazakhstan armed forces kept the Soviet era uniforms and decorations and just replaced the cap badges.

When Padgett and the detachment landed, they went to work with the surgeon operating, often with Padgett standing in as the first assistant, and the dentist working on teeth. The medics helped where they could, slowly winning over the hearts and minds of those they provided medical attention to. After a couple of days the population of the nearby town of Talgy-Hurgan started lining up for general medical consults and that's where Padgett and any free medic spent their time.

On arrival at the military hospital, the detachment was shown its quarters and then asked if it wanted to view the "Best Nurse" competition. This was an annual event, not staged for the detachment's benefit. It was in progress when detachment members took their seats at the hospital auditorium. The officers, like Padgett, were assigned an interpreter to guide them through the proceedings. Padgett's escort was a young lieutenant, who took a seat beside him. The contest was kind of a skill and talent show. The nurses had a talent to demonstrate, such as singing or dancing, etc., and then they were given a timed medical task such as putting on an Ace wrap or sling, etc. The winner would receive a small kitchen appliance and a dozen roses. The wards that put up their nurses to represent them were really into the program.

While Padgett was enjoying the competition, his interpreter, a young ethnic Russian lieutenant, leaned over and asked: "What is that patch on your right sleeve?" Padgett was wearing his battle dress uniform, or fatigues, and explained to the interpreter, "in the American Army we wear the patch of the unit we served in combat with on our right sleeve."

He nodded and queried further, "Special Forces, isn't it?"

"Yes, it is," Padgett replied.

"You were in Vietnam?"

John "Doc" Padgett with his wife Vicki attending the Grand Ball in Vienna in 2015. (Photo Courtesy of John "Doc" Padgett)

"That's right."

"Were you ever in Laos?"

At that point Padgett attempted to change the subject, but the young lieutenant persisted. By 1997, the 20-year classification period that prohibited any SOG Green Beret or support troop from discussing SOG or its missions had passed. But those like Padgett who not only served in SOG but had participated in one of the most successful operations of the eight-year secret war without ever discussing it outside of tight circles with fellow Special Forces troops, were still reluctant to talk about SOG, the secret war and especially Laos.

However, on this day in 1997, it became clear to Padgett that the young host officer had doubtless done his homework on Padgett and Special Forces, so the veteran Green Beret medic quietly affirmed what he assumed the young Russian probably already knew.

Then the young Russian had a surprise for Padgett:

It turned out that his father was a Soviet adviser to North Vietnamese anti-aircraft units stationed along the Ho Chi Minh Trail in Laos. Now, the nurse competition was forgotten, as they started comparing locations in Laos where the Russian artillery officer had served and the dates when he was trying to shoot down U.S. aircraft.

As the discussion went on, Padgett's mind flashed back to September 13, 1970, while flying in the huge Sikorsky Marine Corps CH-53D west, deep into Laos to pick up the most seriously wounded warriors among the B Company men from CCC in Kontum. Padgett's mind vividly remembered seeing anti-aircraft flack exploding in the air around the helicopters: "It was reminiscent of the ack-ack from World War II, like the deadly anti-aircraft guns the Germans used against U.S. planes flying bombing missions over Germany and France. Seeing those ack-ack blasts reminded me of the (post-WW II) films Twelve O'Clock High (starring Gregory Peck) and Command Decision (starring Clark Gable).... I vividly recall going through flack on my way to attempt a rescue of our SOG commandos on Operation Tailwind. It's a day I'll never forget."

With memories of that horrific day still swirling around in his mind, Padgett was astounded that 27 years later he was having a conversation with the son of the man who tried to shoot him down.

There was one aspect of that fateful day that Padgett didn't share with the young Russian officer: As the CH-53D helicopter was descending toward the LZ to pick up the wounded, a piece of enemy shrapnel ripped through the helicopter and became embedded in Padgett's flack vest. "I always wore flack vests after that mission," he said.

Moments later, that helicopter took heavy enemy ground fire and crashed. Those who came to rescue the wounded had to be rescued themselves a short while later by another Marine CH-53D from HMH-463, code named YH-20.

CHAPTER EIGHT

CNN Insults Tailwind Bravery/Valor

CNN: The Fake News Network

Twenty-eight years after one of the most successful operations run in 1970 during the eight-year secret war—Operation Tailwind—CNN broadcast a disgraceful, erroneous story that stained the reputations of the men, who participated in that mission, portraying them as war criminals.

Instead of reporting the facts of the successful mission, CNN accused the Green Berets and airmen of gassing American POWs held captive in Laos with deadly sarin gas.

CNN used that error-laden work of fiction in an effort to compete with CBS's popular 60 Minutes program when it launched a new program on June 7, 1998, called NewsStand.

The title of the bogus, slanderous story was entitled "Valley of Death." It alleged that 16 Green Berets and 120 indigenous troops from Operation Tailwind had destroyed a village and killed innocent women and children while directing U.S. aircraft to drop lethal sarin nerve gas on U.S. war defectors they said were POWs of the communists.

To compound the egregious attack against America's finest soldiers and airmen, the next day, Time Magazine repeated the

Then retired Lt. Col. Gene McCarley stands behind the DoD microphone refuting the scandalous, distorted, report broadcast by CNN and reported in Time Magazine. The DoD, Department of Air Force and Army investigations following the fake news that besmeared and denigrated one of the most successful operations in SOG's eight-year history completely vindicated the actions of the airmen and soldiers involved in Operation Tailwind. (Photo Courtesy of Gene McCarley)

hideous allegations in a news story written by CNN staff members headlined: "Did the U.S. Drop Nerve Gas?" It was written by CNN Producer April Oliver and CNN international correspondent Peter Arnett, who produced the CNN story that aired June 7th.

The broadcast and Time article smeared the men of Operation Tailwind, which was conducted during the eight-year secret war in Laos during the Vietnam War, and run under the aegis of the Military Assistance Command Vietnam—Studies and Observations Group, or simply SOG.

Operation Tailwind was conducted south of the Bolovens Plateau in southern Laos 47 years ago. Led by Green Beret Capt. Gene McCarley, 15 Green Berets and 120 Montagnard mercenaries executed a hair-raising, four-day mission deep inside enemy territory to take the pressure off of a CIA operation further west in Laos dubbed Operation Gauntlet, with a diversionary operation along Highway 165 on the plateau against the communist North Vietnamese Army (NVA). Operation Tailwind not only succeeded in diverting NVA assets and hundreds of soldiers from the CIA battlefield, but it netted one of the largest intelligence coups by a Green Beret team in the secret war's history.

Operation Tailwind went down in the annals of SOG history as one of the most successful operations because of its unique nature and because it was conducted beyond the area authorized for routine SOG operations in Laos. And, because that operation was part of the secret war, its success could not be discussed beyond closed circles of participants and only military brass who had a Top Secret clearance and a need to know. It was so secret that the awards and decorations earned by soldiers, Marines, and Air Force airmen, said the valorous actions occurred in the Republic of S. Vietnam.

Operation Tailwind was a success in large part due to the aggressive leadership of McCarley, a SOG veteran who had run SOG reconnaissance missions into Laos, and the relentless day-and-night air cover provided to the Green Berets by Air Force SPADs, F-4 Phantom jets, C-119K Stingers, C-130E Spectre gunships, Marine Corps Cobra gunships and heavy transport CH-

After the formal press conference, the Green Berets SOG Commanders and key participants from Operation Tailwind gathered for a photo op with then-Secretary of Defense William S. Cohen, in the Pentagon in 1998. From left: Col. (Ret.) John "Skip" Sadler, his title was Chief SOG in 1970, he was the officer in charge of SOG missions, Lt. Col. (Ret.) Gene McCarley, he was commander of the B Company Hatchet Force that launched into Laos with 16 Green Berets, 120 Montagnards, Cohen, Green Beret medic Gary Mike Rose, and Col. (Ret.) Bob Pinkerton, who was the operations officers at SOG Headquarters in Saigon during Operation Tailwind. (Photo Courtesy of Gene McCarley)

53D Sikorsky helicopters.

Green Berets who served on the secret mission from Sept. 11–14, 1970, Air Force, Marine and Army aviators, who flew in support of Operation Tailwind, said that when they were initially interviewed by CNN, they were told the story would focus on the mission. However, during the interviews, the reporters would often raise questions about the use of sarin gas and if they had killed women and children and American war defectors.

"CNN, when faced with an amazing story of courage, daring and military success maligned the brave soldiers, Marines and airmen who brilliantly fought the assigned mission against staggering odds," said Houston-based attorney Jim Moriarty, a Vietnam veteran who served three tours of duty with Marine Corps aviation, which included supporting missions across the fence into Laos.

"CNN chose to invent their preconceived narrative, one utterly lacking in credible evidence," he said. "And, CNN worked hard to avoid reporting on the credible evidence that showed no use of sarin nerve gas nor any intent to kill American Defectors...(also) CNN ignored its in-house military advisor."

Retired Air Force Maj. Gen. Perry Smith was that highly regarded military analyst to whom Moriarty referred. Smith had been on retainer by CNN since the Persian Gulf War in August 1990. He had authored a book "How CNN Fought The War—A View From The Inside," which detailed CNN's 24-hour coverage of the Persian Gulf War. It explained how CNN set new standards of war correspondence in the rapidly expanding field of electronic news.

Smith is highly respected for his work there and as an Air Force fighter pilot and commander of airmen. In his book he detailed how CNN reporters were in Baghdad on Jan. 16, 1991 when U.S. air strikes commenced and how the cable network quickly surpassed ABC, CBS and NBC with its 24-hour-a-day war coverage, complete with reports from on the ground in Baghdad. Smith documents CNN's ground-breaking journalistic trend at a time when there was no cable or regular television network doing news 24 hours a day, unlike 2017 when there is a myriad of cable and satellite choices and dozens of pretend or self-proclaimed news experts blogging away merrily with little fact or knowledge of history.

In June 1998, Smith only learned about the "Valley of Death" story the Wednesday before it aired on CNN June 7, 1998. "I found out on Wednesday.... I did a little research. I talked to April Oliver and Jack Smith, I told them that couldn't happen. I told them the Air Force wouldn't use nerve gas. It was against our Rules of Engagement. I tried very hard to stop it. But, they had done promos on it and they had hired Rick Kaplan to kick up the ratings, so he thought they had a really juicy story.... I felt sick to my stomach watching it when it aired."

Smith tried "very hard for a week to convince" top CNN executives to do a major retraction and issue an apology. "Lots of people at CNN were solidly with me on this, but not the top bosses and the team that put that terrible special together."

Twenty-four hours after "Valley of Death" aired, Smith had contacted Air Force ordnance personnel who confirmed that the only sarin nerve gas supply in 1970 was held at six military installations: four in U.S. bases, one in Germany and one in Okinawa—there was no sarin gas anywhere in Southeast Asia in 1970. None. Zero. A stark fact CNN failed to report.

During that first week after the June 7, 1998 broadcast, Smith called McCarley and told him that he had received a letter from a veteran telling him he had to go public with his concerns about the biased, inaccurate report. When CNN executives refused to issue an apology or a retraction, and instead broadcast a lame follow-up story on June 14, Smith resigned in protest, hoping his resignation would finally get some attention at the highest levels of CNN management. He wrote a piece for the N.Y. Times Business section expressing his concerns about the piece, he appeared with Charlie Rose for 20 minutes, and he offered to cooperate with respected First Amendment attorney Floyd Abrams when the media lawyer was commissioned to head a panel to investigate veterans' complaints of gross inaccuracies and false, fabricated information that CNN broadcast. After

Smith surfaced publicly, he received more than 2,000 letters and e-mails from veterans and citizens angered by the story.

Serious Consequences of False Reporting

There was an additional political ramification stemming from the CNN/Time report in 1998: "Great harm resulted to the strategic interest of the United States from CNN airing these demonstrably false claims," said Moriarty. "...In 1998 the weapons inspectors were thrown out of Iraq with Iraq claiming that we were hypocrites for accusing them of using chemical weapons against their own people when we had supposedly done the same thing decades earlier (in Laos)...."

At a July 21, 1998 press conference repudiating the CNN/Time report, then-Secretary of Defense William Cohen said, "... The charge would be used to discredit the United States' attempt to curb the proliferation of weapons of mass destruction. In fact, Iraq immediately incorporated CNN's charges into its anti-U.S. propaganda campaign in an effort to try to deflect attention from its own outlawed chemical and biological weapons programs..."

Cohen ordered a full-scale, across the boards investigation of the CNN/Time story from all military branches involved in Operation Tailwind, while requesting the same from the CIA and the Joint Chiefs of Staff.

New York Times Columnist William Safire wrote at that time: "Though not so intended, this questionable report about poison-gas use—slyly cast as an accusing question in Time's headline—will reinforce CNN's favored access to facilities in Baghdad at a critical moment."

For the Green Berets who ran the mission on the ground and for the fearless aviators who supported them, including A-1H Skyraider pilots who dropped tear gas on the enemy during mortal combat in Laos, not deadly sarin nerve gas, the CNN/Time story implied that they were war criminals.

McCarley was working with a private security firm when the show was broadcast. "I was busy working, saw glimpses of it...I didn't like what I saw. You could tell they were manipulating, cutting people's quotes to fit their story line."

During Operation Tailwind, the only Green Beret medic on the ground was Sgt. Gary Mike Rose. He, along with the remaining 15 Green Berets, suffered varying degrees of combat wounds from shrapnel to gunshot. During the DoD probe of the CNN/Time story Rose told investigators, "I'm living proof that toxic gas was not dropped on us that day. Nobody showed any signs of exposure to toxic gas. Had there been sarin gas used, all of us would have died."

Additionally, he added, "If toxic gas had been used, there would have been stacks of dead NVA soldiers — all of whom were trying to kill us [on final extraction from the LZ], the Green Berets and many of our indigenous troops...Yet, when that show aired, I had to turn to my 20-year-old daughter and explain that I had done nothing wrong. That hurt."

Sgt. Mike Hagen said, "We call it the Communist News Network to this day because when I heard CNN was going to do a story on Tailwind, I gathered the family around the television and tuned it in for us to watch. Imagine my horror, my utter and complete horror when I was sitting there with my family and I was portrayed as a fucking war criminal...I never got over that."

Retractions and Apologies

At a July 21, 1998 press conference, after military staff worked more than 1,700 hours investigating CNN/Time's error-laden story, Secretary Cohen said, "I think all Americans should know that the 16 men who conducted this mission were heroes, but they have been hurt by this report...I can assure you and your colleagues and your families, you did nothing wrong. Quite to the contrary, you did everything right. Sixteen Americans fought steadily for four days. All of them were injured. All got out alive. The documents that they captured provided an intelligence bonanza...General Abrams, the commander of our troops in Vietnam, said Tailwind was a valuable operation executed with great skill and tremendous courage."

Cohen told reporters that after rigorous review of thousands of pages of documents, statements, after-action reports, and military ordinance and weapons storage records, "We found no evidence to support CNN/Time assertions. We have found absolutely no evidence to support these charges…CNN and Time retracted their reports, noting that they could not support either charge."

On July 2, 1998, in a CNN retraction, CNN News Group Chairman, President and CEO Tom Johnson said an independent investigation concluded that the report "cannot be supported. There was insufficient evidence that sarin or any other deadly gas was used and CNN could not confirm that American defectors were targeted or at the camp as NewsStand reported…. We apologize to our viewers and to our colleagues at Time for this mistake. CNN owes a special apology to the personnel involved in Operation Tailwind, both the soldiers on the ground and the U.S. Air Force pilots and U.S. Marine Corps helicopter pilots who were involved in this action."

On July 13th, Time magazine printed an apology to its readers, headlined "Tailwind: An Apology." It noted that the allegations reported on June 7th and 8th, 1998 could not be "supported by the evidence."

In a July 14, 1998 letter, Ted Turner wrote to McCarley, "…I hope you will accept my personal apology for CNN NewsStand's recent erroneous reporting on Operation Tailwind. This entire episode has been very painful for me as the founder of CNN. However, my greatest distress comes from knowing that our coverage upset those on the front line of Operation Tailwind—the soldiers on the ground and the U.S. Air Force and U.S. Marine Corps pilots engaged in the action."

McCarley said in a 2015 interview, "I spoke personally to Ted Turner and he reiterated what he wrote in the letter. He also told me he was going to call the other members of our team and write them letters of apology. To the best of my knowledge that didn't happen."

Larry Groah, a Marine Corps helicopter door gunner who survived Operation Tailwind added: "I really felt betrayed by CNN for allowing those reporters to publish all those lies and twisting the statements from those who were interviewed. CNN really showed me how the news media can twist a story to fit its needs and I've never really trusted any of the other media 100 percent in their reporting since then."

Interviewed in 2016, retired Air Force Lt. Col. Mel Swanson, who was the commanding officer of the daring A-1 Skyraider pilots, remained brutally bitter about CNN's false story. "Operation Tailwind was the classic example of inter-service cooperation in the Area of Operations. Think about it: America's finest, the Green Berets and their loyal troops kicked ass and took numbers on the ground, deep in enemy territory. The Tactical Air support from Air Force fastmovers, C-130 gunships, our beloved (A-1H) SPADs, in combination with Marine Corps Scarface Cobra gunships, Army Cobras and Marine Corps Dimmers raised hell in the enemy's back yard. We killed hundreds of those commie bastards, and thanks to that Green Beret medic, all were kept alive until the final extraction when one Montagnard soldier was killed.... Until 1998, I occasionally watched the Communist New Network, but after they ruined our reputations, I never watched it again. It was a crime against warriors, what they did. It was a travesty of justice."

CHAPTER NINE

Postscript: Operation Tailwind

There are contingent liabilities for those who fight in secret wars.

For the Green Berets, their fearless indigenous forces, and the courageous aviators from the Army, Air Force and Marine Corps who supported the airborne soldiers during the eight-year secret war across the fence in Laos, Cambodia and North Vietnam there are haunting repercussions from it.

When the Green Berets signed federal documents pledging not to talk to their mothers, girlfriends or anyone without a "need to know" for 20 years about SOG's secret war, few if any ever thought about:

- What would their parents be told if they were killed in action in Laos, Cambodia or N. Vietnam?
- What would the U.S. government say publicly, if anything, if they were killed in action in the "neutral countries" of Laos and Cambodia, or communist-held N. Vietnam?
- What would their parents be told if they went missing in action in those "neutral countries?"
- What would be said if they received the nation's highest valor award, the Medal of Honor for combat in those two "neutral countries?"

- And, what, as in the case of Operation Tailwind, would the country be told if anything, about one of the most successful and heroic operations in SOG's secret history?

The quick answer: The government would lie, deny or simply not acknowledge where the Green Berets died, where they fought heroically or where they went missing in action.

Why?

When fighting a secret war the government needs plausible deniability, as documented earlier in the book.

And, there's one additional oddity of fighting in a secret war, where strictly compartmentalized entities exist to protect secrets, both operational and political. That compartmentalization trickles down into SOG Recon and Hatchet Force companies, where men on the ground often can't/don't talk about exact missions, or where they ran top-secret missions into Laos, Cambodia or N. Vietnam. That oddity was further compounded by the fact that the typical tour of duty in Vietnam lasted for one year, thus yielding a high turnover ratio. Then you add the Green Berets killed in action, missing in action, wounded in action or sent home due to one of the many jungle-related ailments easily contracted, difficult to rid. And there was little historical information between teams and team leaders. Unspoken, there often was a consistent turnover among indigenous personnel too.

Thus no hand off of historical knowledge about the Area of Operations, or of risky missions conducted in the past, and then reassigned to another Recon Team later, without the benefit of prior experiences being conveyed to the next team leader.

Last, but certainly not least, seldom – if ever - would a SOG Recon Team or Hatchet Force Green Beret have an opportunity to meet, let alone personally thank, the aviator who had just put their life on the line against withering enemy gunfire and anti-aircraft weapons to make it possible for a troop-carrying helicopter to land and pick up the SOG personnel on the ground. Or, more dangerously, hover for several minutes while suppressing enemy gunfire as helicopter crew members dropped 150-foot-long rope to the jungle floor for the ground pounders to hook up and be slowly lifted out of the jungle: in Laos, that would generally mean going through triple-canopy vegetation that grew 100-plus feet from terra firma.

The classic example of aviators paying the supreme price to save a recon team is Part Two, *Still Searching for SOG MIAs*. Four aviators from Company A (the Comancheros) of the 101st Aviation Battalion, 101st Airborne Division of Camp Eagle, Phu Bai, died with two RT Intruder recon Green Berets in a horrific, crushing crash after communist gunners hammered the Screaming Eagle's Huey chopper as it lifted out the two soldiers from deep jungle vegetation in Laos. The next day, after a recon team was inserted to locate their bodies, a small Air Force O-2A Cessna observation plane crashed while helping that team locate the six dead Americans. The pilot and Special Forces observer died in the crash after being hit by heavy communist ground fire. One mission, three Green Berets, six 101st Airborne aviators, killed in action.

Among the aviators most seldom seen by the Green Berets on the ground were the Air Force pilots who flew the supersonic Phantom F-4 jet, the prop-driven A-1 Skyraider and the powerful Jolly Green Giant heavy-lift Sikorsky helicopters – their motto: "That Others May Live."

By comparison, there were a few occasions when certain helicopter crews would be regularly assigned to a SOG base, such as in July 1968, when the legendary 176th Gunships of 36-c, the Muskets from the Americal Division were based at FOB 1 in Phu Bai. The SeaBees built a special barracks where they resided over night and developed a strong rapport with the SF men in camp. The Air Force's 20th Special Operations Squadron, the Green Hornets were regularly assigned to FOB 5 and FOB 6 in S. Vietnam, thus the operators got to know them on a first-name basis. But, those were unique situations.

Returning to Operation Tailwind, none of the air assets were based at CCC – formerly FOB 2 in Kontum — or at the SOG launch site for that compound at Dak To.

One week after the conclusion of Operation Tailwind, Marine Corps and Army aviators held a celebration at CCC in Kontum with the Green Berets who ran that historic, top secret mission and other Special Forces personnel assigned to the top secret base in the Central Highlands. (Photo Courtesy of Barry Pencek)

A few days after all of the men who fought on the ground and in the air on Operation Tailwind successfully returned to their respective home bases, McCarley and the command staff at CCC threw a party to celebrate the successful mission as details began to surface about the nature and depth of the intelligence coup Company B men pulled off when they seized so many NVA documents, maps, etc., from the last NVA base camp that they left in smoke and ashes in Laos. There aren't a lot of details about the celebration, but it's generally agreed that many participants drank an excess of alcohol.

That was a unique experience in and of itself, even though someone forgot to invite the SPAD pilots. Thus, the operational tempo impeded the development of camaraderie between the men on the ground and those who died supporting them. After a mission, the wounded troops would be treated by SF medics or at the nearest military hospital, the team leader would give the intelligence team the latest word in a formal debriefing from the Area of Operations and that target, while the air crews returned to their respective bases to refuel, reload and repair their aircraft.

This was the norm in the SOG secret war: valor, heroism, courage, bravery under intense enemy fire – every mission, every target. Then return to base.

Fast forward to 2013, after a few phone calls, former A1-H Skyraider pilot Don Engebretsen, who flew SOG and Search and Rescue missions with the 56th Special Operations Wing, Operating Location Alpha Alpha in Da Nang, contacted Special Operations Association Membership Committee Chairman Ray Calafell in Tampa, inquiring about the veterans group formed by SOG recon men in 1976 which expanded to include aviation units that supported SOG missions. Because of the SPADs' unique unit designation (OLAA) and Air Force assignment in 1969, Calafell – a combat Vietnam veteran – asked Engebretsen the first obvious question: "You flew support for SOG? Geez, I know SPADs supported SOG missions, Ranger missions and tradition units in Vietnam, but I never heard what their designation was…. Let me make a few phone calls."

Calafell and Engebretsen teamed up to make a formal

On Day 3 of Operation Tailwind, Sept. 13, 1970, Marine Corps Sgt. Ron Whitmer, left and Sgt. Larry Groah were door gunners on the CH-53D heavy-lift helicopter, YH-20 that rescued the crew and Green Beret medics from YH-14 after it crash landed while attempting to pick up the most seriously wounded soldiers from the mission in Laos. Whitmer was the right-side gunner while Groah manned the left side, where he eliminated an enemy 51-caliber heavy machine gun position and gunner that had opened up on the Dimmer as it was descending into the landing zone.

Whitmer and Groah were presented with the CCC patches at the post-Operation Tailwind party that was held at CCC in Kontum one week after the successful mission. After the Green Berets presented the CCC patches to Whitmer and Groah, "they told us to not wear those whenever we went across the fence into Laos on any SOG mission as there was a bounty on anyone wearing it and, if caught, our heads would be placed on a pole. Scary stuff," said Groah in a 2017 interview. This photo was taken at their base in Da Nang outside Marble Mountain.
(Photo Courtesy of Larry Groah)

presentation to the SOA Board of Directors. The board approved the OLAA pilots as new members of the association in time for them to attend the SOA's annual fall reunion in Las Vegas.

"I'll never forget the reunion of 2013," said Doug LeTourneau, who ran SOG missions on recon teams Virginia and Idaho at FOB 1/CCN 68-69. "Over the years we never had the opportunity to put a face to the pilot of the A1 Skyraider who always put their lives on the line to save and protect our recon teams.... I can't tell you how many times SPADs supported my team on the ground during my one year (in country). They went back to their base, we went back to our base and got ready for the next mission. (After their tour of duty) they went home, we went home and got on with life. At the (SOA) reunion, to be able to shake the hands of the men who supported us in the Prairie Fire AO was a gratifying and yes, emotional moment in time for me. I'll never forget it. Every year since, it just gets better at each reunion, hearing their stories."

Engebretsen said that first reunion was "life changing" for him, "profoundly rewarding" because he met Green Berets who appreciated that he and fellow A-1 pilots had supported SOG teams on the ground from the air with deadly precision and courage which led to them being extracted from the target.

"Our unit was sworn to the same 'secrecy' requirements as all SOG participants, so we came home, kept our mouths shut, and never considered that those restrictions were lifted nor that SOG members were having well-organized, open gatherings. We were welcomed by the SOA like lost brothers and the magic began. We brought a lot of mission information – which contained specific dated missions, locations in many cases actual mission co-ordinates, team code names, FAC call signs, BDA (Bomb Damage Assessments), etc. – and began the process of exchanging how we operated in our respective roles. I met two men involved on my RT Vermont mission and some of our other pilots began making contacts with team members they actually supported as well. The emotions ran strong and deep...."

Following that reunion, some of the pilots learned that an A1-H

Skyraider flown in the secret war, was still flying from the Tennessee Museum of Aviation in Sevierville, TN. The following year, Engebretsen and a few other SPAD pilots went to the airport, saw the A1-H – tail number 665 – and held a small, impromptu gathering. At the 2014 SOA reunion Engebretsen, a few of his fellow SPAD pilots and SOA leadership began planning events at the unique museum.

In 2015, the SPAD pilots held a reunion to honor Brigadier General James W. "Jim" Wold, commanding officer for the 6th Special Operation Squadron in Pleiku and later assumed command of Operating Location Alpha Alpha (OLAA) units at Pleiku and Da Nang air bases, which supported SOG and SAR missions. Wold was honored during a special reunion at the museum.

Next year, the first Operation Tailwind Reunion was held at the Tennessee Museum of Aviation, bringing together for the first time in more than 45 years some of the men from all of the aviations units and some of the Special Forces soldiers from that unique mission – featuring B Company Commanding Officer, Gene McCarley; the commanding officer of the A-1 Skyraiders from OLAA, Mel Swanson; and pilots who flew Marine Corps Cobra gunships from Scarface, the heavy-lift CH-53D Sikorsky Dimmers pilots and a few forward air controllers.

With tears in his eyes, Swanson said, "I hope this is the first of more reunions like it. To see how grateful the men of SOG were for our support during those hairy Prairie Fire missions touches me through and through, as well as the other pilots here today. We always wondered who those crazy fuckers on the ground were and now, thanks to the SOA reunions – and this reunion – we get to meet them. And, I can't tell you how much this means to me on a personal level, as the commander who sent our A-1 pilots into harm's way every day, to now learn how much they appreciated us in the AO… it's gratifying beyond words."

During that reunion there was a panel featuring McCarley, Swanson, and several of the pilots who participated in Operation Tailwind. Some of the key points mentioned during that two-plus hour discussion were:

- McCarley pointed out that SF medic Gary Mike Rose was wounded three times.
- Dimmer pilot Don Persky, said he and a 22-year-old first lieutenant pilot of the final CH-53D were lifting off from the LZ on Day 4, when the heavy-lift helicopter took numerous hits from enemy fire: "Our (helicopter) chin was going through the trees, just barely getting enough translational lift to transition from hover to full flight," he said.
- Persky was one of several pilots who remembered seeing the anti-aircraft ack-ack exploding in the air while flying to and from the LZ – just as Doc Padgett had seen it.
- Dimmer Pilot Mark McKenzie, who picked up the SF and air crew from Dimmer YH-14 that crashed on Day Three, turned toward the SOG Green Berets in the audience and said, "I respect you guys, but you know what, you guys are crazy." That comment drew a round of laughs from everyone.
- SPAD Pilot Don Feld said he could hear the Tailwind operations on the ground "puking, choking, gagging on the radio from the CS (tear gas he dropped on Day Four).... It sounded like he was dying." During one gun run his engine started to sound funny, so he turned toward Da Nang, which was closer than his base in Thailand. By the time he landed, "one piston was banging around pretty bad. The engine was ready to crap out." He was glad to make it back in one piece.
- Scarface Pilot Barry Pencek brought some fact-laced humor to the event. He told the audience that when the Marines went across the fence into Laos, "They made us change our call sign for some reason – they called them Mission 72 when we went across the fence. Whenever we ran a Mission 72, for some

reason, they had us take off our dog tags, leave our wallet at home so you couldn't be identified – as if you go down in an American-made helicopter, and you're a white guy, round eye in an Asian country, and nobody is going to know you're an American!! I never understood the logic of that."

- On a serious note, Pencek said that he obtained copies of formerly highly classified radio traffic years later that documented 1970 scuttlebutt about the Marine Corps "not being thrilled" about having six of its entire fleet of 24 Cobras and six of the Dimmers dedicated to Operation Tailwind "which was half of the grand total the Marine Corps had in Vietnam at that time (1970). The generals were yelling back and forth against each other." He said it was funny reading communications between high-ranking generals complaining about the high proportion of assets used in Operation Tailwind. In the end, five Dimmers and six Scarface Cobras were assigned to the operation. Swanson quipped an aside: "Hell the Marine brass wasn't too happy about losing two Dimmers, until they learned about the sensational success of the joint mission."

- Then, on an impromptu closing note – that seemed to be an apropos editorial comment on Operation Tailwind in general laced in the vernacular of 1970 – Pencek turned to the audience and apologized to the ladies in advance for "contaminating" the spoken word with profanities to summarize the time he spent during that operation.

"I can't think of another way to say this," he said, apologetically.

"For example, if somebody is really good, he's a hot shit.

"If something was good, it was shit hot.

"If you got into a bad situation, it was a shit sandwich. Don (Persky) mentioned the sandwich we got into (earlier).

"If you had your act together you had your shit together.

"And, I would like to say that I was honored to have a week or so to spend with all of these people here and a bunch of others, and they were a bunch of hot-shit guys, on a shit-hot mission, and we got into a shit sandwich but, we had our shit together in the end... no shit!!!

Indeed, that's a classic, albeit somewhat shitty postscript to Operation Tailwind.

This is a link to a video of the Tailwind panel at Tennessee Museum of Aviation:
https://vimeo.com/166371295

***

Awards and Decorations

A listing of awards and decorations received by Operation Tailwind participants:

The Green Berets of B Company Hatchet Force, MACV-SOG Command and Control Central (CCC):

CCC, Company B, Headquarters Section
Commanding Officer Capt. **Gene McCarley**
    – Silver Star, two Purple Hearts.

Medic Sgt. **Gary Mike Rose**
    – Medal of Honor, Distinguished Service Cross, three Purple Hearts.

Company First Sergeant, Master Sgt. **Morris Adair**
    – Bronze Star w/a "V" Device for Valor, two Purple Hearts.

This is a photo of Gary Mike Rose shortly after he enlisted in the army before going to Special Forces training. (Photo Courtesy of Gary Mike Rose.)

First Platoon

Platoon Leader, 1st Lt. **Bob Van Buskirk**
   – Silver Star, two Purple Hearts.

Platoon, Sgt., First Class **Jim Brevelle**
   – Bronze Star w/a "V" Device for Valor, one Purple Heart.

Squad Leader, Sgt. **Manuel Orozco**
   – Silver Star, one Purple Heart.

Squad Leader, Specialist 5th Class **Craig Schmidt**
   – Silver Star, three Purple Hearts.

Squad Leader, Staff Sgt. **William Sherer**
   – Bronze Star w/a "V" Device for Valor, one Purple Heart.

Second Platoon

Platoon Leader, 1st Lt. **Peter "Hippie" Landon**
   – Bronze Star w/a "V" Device for Valor, one Purple Heart.

Squad Leader, Sgt. **Keith Plancich**
   – Bronze Star w/a "V" Device for Valor, three Purple Hearts.

Squad Leader, Sgt. First Class **Denver Minton**
   – Bronze Star w/a "V" Device for Valor.

Squad Leader 2nd Platoon, Sgt. **Mike Hagen**
   – Bronze Star w/a "V" Device for Valor, one Purple Heart.

Third Platoon

Platoon Leader, Sgt. First Class **Bernie Bright**
   – Bronze Star w/a "V" Device for Valor, three Purple Hearts.

Platoon Leader, Sgt. **Dave Young**
   – Bronze Star w/a "V" Device for Valor, one Purple Heart.

Platoon Leader, Specialist Fifth Class **James D. Lucas**
   – Silver Star, one Purple Heart.

Platoon Leader, Sgt. **Donald Boudreau**
   – Bronze Star w/a "V" Device for Valor, two Purple Hearts.

Operation Tailwind's sole Green Beret medic was Gary Mike Rose, pictured here receiving the Distinguished Service Cross from General Creighton Abrams, the top military officer in Vietnam in early 1971. (Photo Courtesy of Gary Mike Rose)

This is a photo of A-1H Skyraider, tail number 665, flying over Southeast Asia during the Vietnam War, carrying a full load of ordnance, including 2.75 rockets. (Photo Courtesy of Don Engebretsen)

Other CCC Special Forces Tailwind Support
Awards and Decorations

Medic Staff Sgt. **John F. Browne** – Air Medal for Valor (from Day 3).

Medic Staff Sgt. **John "Doc" Padgett** – Air Medal for Valor (Day 3).

Medic Staff Sgt. **Randall G. Shockey** – Purple Heart (Day 3).

Radio Operator Sgt. First Class **Roy L. Myers** – Purple Heart (Day 3).

Air Force 56th Special Operations Wing, Operating Location
Alpha Alpha (OLAA) A-1 Skyraiders based in Da Nang.

Lt. Col. **Melvin G. Swanson** – Distinguished Flying Cross.

Capt. **Levy M. Rentz, Jr**. – Distinguished Flying Cross.

Capt. **Dick Kent** – Distinguished Flying Cross.

1st Lt. **Thomas K. Stump** – Distinguished Flying Cross.

1st Lt. **Chris M. Tateishi** – Distinguished Flying Cross.

1st Lt. **Charles "Chuck" Kasbeer** – Distinguished Flying Cross.

Marine Corps HML-367 (Scarface)
Cobra Gunship based in Da Nang

Lt. Col. **Harry Sexton,** Overall Aviation Operations Commander
– Navy Cross

First Lt. **Sid Baker**, Section Leader – Silver Star.

First Lt. **Joseph Driscoll** – Distinguished Flying Cross.

First Lt. **Barry Pencek** – Distinguished Flying Cross.

First Lt. **Pat Owen** – Distinguished Flying Cross.

First Lt. **Ed "Dink" Crowe** – Distinguished Flying Cross.

First Lt. **Rob Robinette** – Distinguished Flying Cross.

First Lt. **Robert Grove** – Distinguished Flying Cross.

First Lt. **Joseph Gallo** – Purple Heart.

On Oct. 23, 2017 President Donald J. Trump presented Green Beret Medic Gary Mike Rose the Medal of Honor in recognition of his valor during Operation Tailwind. His wife Margaret, 11 Green Berets and aviators from the original mission attended the formal ceremony in the East Wing of the White House. (Photo Courtesy of DOD)

Other Scarface Operation Tailwind Citations

Sgt. **R.W. Remer** (avionics), Sgt. **Bentlinger** and Cpl. **Randall** (metal shop) received written citations for their work repairing and rearming the Marine Cobras.

Marine Corps HMH-463 Heavy-Lift CH-53D Helicopters (Dimmers)

First Lt. **Donald N. Persky**
 – Silver Star for Conspicuous Gallantry/Intrepidity in action.

First Lt. **Mark McKenzie**
 – Distinguished Flying Cross for Heroism/Extraordinary Achievement in Aerial Flight.

Sergeant **Larry A. Groah II**
 – Air Medal with Bronze Star for "Heroic Achievement".

First Lt. **Raul H. Bustamante**
 – Air Medal with Bronze Star for "Heroic Achievement".

Lt. Col. **Robert R. Leisy**
 – Air Medal with Bronze Star for "Heroic Achievement".

First Lt. **Willis H. Beardall**
 – Air Medal with Bronze Star for Heroism/Extraordinary Achievement in Aerial Flight.

Capt. **Arthur J. Picone Jr**.
 – Air Medal with Bronze Star for Heroism/Extraordinary Achievement in Aerial Flight.

Sergeant **Carlton E. Meng**
 – Air Medal with Bronze Star for "Heroic Achievement".

Capt. **Henry J. "Chip" Cipolla**
 – Bronze Star for Heroic Achievement, a Gold Star representing his second Bronze Star award.

After the panel discussion on April 30, 2016 on Operation Tailwind at the Tennessee Museum of Aviation, the veterans who served in that mission gathered for group photo in front of the A1-H Skyraider, Tail Number 665, which was flown in support of top secret mission in Laos during the secret war.

From left: Bill Beardall, Marine Corps HMH-463 CH-53D "Dimmer" Pilot; Larry Smith, USAF 21st TASS PFE FAC OV-10 "Covey 566" Pilot; Barry Pencek, Marine Corps HML-367 AH-1G Cobra "Scarface" Pilot; Joe Driscoll, Marine Corps HML-367 AH-1G Cobra "Scarface" Pilot; Bernie Bright, Army SOG "Operation Tailwind" Company B, 3rd Platoon Leader Craig Schmidt, Army SOG "Operation Tailwind" Company B, Squad Leader; Tom Stump, USAF OLAA A-1 Skyraider "Spad" Pilot; Gene McCarley, Army SOG "Operation Tailwind" Commander and Company B commanding officer; Don Persky, Marine HMH-463 CH-53D "Dimmer" Pilot; Mel Swanson, USAF OLAA A-1 Skyraider "Spad" Commander; Mark McKenzie, MARINE HMH-463 CH-53D "Dimmer" Pilot, Don Feld, USAF 56th SOW A-1 Skyraider "Hobo" Pilot; Levy Rentz, USAF OLAA A-1 Skyraider "Spad" Pilot; and Chuck Kasbeer, USAF OLAA A-1 Skyraider "Spad" Pilot.

(Photo Courtesy of Tennessee Museum of Aviation)

During the first Operation Tailwind Reunion held at the Tennessee Museum of Aviation in Seiverville, TN, there was a panel discussion about the historic mission lead by the author John Stryker Meyer. To his right is Mel Swanson, Gene McCarley and Tom Stump. To the left of Meyer is, pilots Larry Smith, Don Persky and Mark McNamara. (Photo Courtesy of Brad Welker)

PART II

Near the top of that distant mountain peak in Laos is the crash site where members of RT Intruder perished in 1971. This photo was taken from an LZ in 2015, which shows how far away the crash site was from where this photo was taken. DPAA officials were unable to get closer to the crash site when this photo was taken in 2015. Efforts continue with Laotian officials to have an LZ closer to the crash site where six Americans from that mission died in one helicopter crash, and two others died one day later helping a SOG recon team locate the RT Intruder crash site. Newman was a member of that recovery team, RT Habu for that mission. He knew all of the Green Berets killed at both crash sites. (Photo Courtesy of Cliff Newman)

CHAPTER TEN

Still Searching For MIAs

RT Intruder: Still MIA 46 years later

Editor's note: *For each edition of SOG Chronicles, there will be a story about a SOG recon team that went missing in action during the eight-year secret war in Laos, Cambodia or N. Vietnam, and remains missing in action when this story was written. As of June 13, 2017, there were still 50 Green Berets listed as MIA in Laos alone, along with at least 105 aviators who died supporting SOG missions. They are among the total of approximately 260 aviators missing in Laos as of this printing.*

Laos is a dramatically different country today than it was 46 years ago when recon teams were running clandestine, top-secret missions there across the fence during the secret war that was fought for 8 years under the aegis of the Military Assistance Command Vietnam – Studies and Observations Group, or simply SOG. In particular, the A Shau Valley—which now has at least one hotel near the A Loui airstrip—was a hotbed of enemy activity throughout the Vietnam War.

John Stryker Meyer

In the early days of the Vietnam War, three Green Beret A-camps were driven from the A Shau Valley between 1965 and '66. Although communists in North Vietnam had signed a treaty in 1962 agreeing not to station or train soldiers in Laos and Cambodia, by 1971 there were more than 60,000 communist soldiers and couriers in Laos alone. The A Shau Valley bristled with NVA armaments, food supplies and equipment delivered to North Vietnam by Russia, China and other Eastern Bloc countries.

At that time, captured enemy documents revealed that the communist North Vietnamese Army (NVA) placed nearly a dozen counter-recon companies in that valley to reinforce LZ (landing zone) watchers and to force locals to work with the communist soldiers. In addition, enemy estimates of troop strength in the A Shau Valley listed several infantry battalions as resting and training there. The communists also moved at least two anti-aircraft artillery (AAA) battalions to defend the valley.

On February 18, 1971, two recon teams assigned to SOG base of operations in Da Nang, Command and Control North (CCN), were designated to run a diversionary mission along the A Shau Valley. Their mission was to tie down NVA enemy forces through the use of air strikes while gathering any military intelligence possible from enemy soldiers, local Laotians pressed into service with the NVA, or through wiretaps.

Because of the dangerous nature of this mission, two additional Green Berets were assigned to RT Intruder: SFC Sammy Hernandez and SFC Charles "Wes" Wesley. The team leader was Capt. Ronald L. "Doc" Watson, the assistant team leader was Sgt. Allen R. "Baby Jesus" Lloyd, and Sgt. Raymond L. "Robby" Robinson was the radio operator. RT Python, with team leader Capt. Jim Butler, was inserted on the eastern side of the A Shau Valley.

Both teams were inserted without incident. RT Intruder, with five Green Berets and five Bru Montagnard team members, moved off the LZ in search of a trail that was near a ridgeline. After moving for a short while, with NVA trackers moving behind them firing signal shots into the air, RT Intruder came across a large trail, crossed it,

146

set up a team security perimeter, and took note of about a dozen separate communications lines lying on the wide trail.

As the team worked with the forward air controller—codenamed Covey—to determine if it was on the correct hill, five enemy soldiers moved down the trail hunting for the team. After a brief firefight, which killed the five NVA soldiers, team leader (One-Zero) Capt. Watson called for an extraction because the team had been compromised. Wesley and Hernandez had also recovered several NVA documents, medals, clothing, and a communist flag from the dead soldiers. They stuffed the spoils of war into a rucksack.

As the team waited for helicopters from Company A (the Comancheros) of the 101st Aviation Battalion, 101st Airborne Division of Camp Eagle, Phu Bai, bad weather started to close in on the ridgeline and the team's LZ. The first chopper started to lift Wesley, Robinson, and two Bru team members out of the LZ when it began to lose power. The four men jumped from the ladder they had started to climb, landing on the dead NVA soldiers they had killed a few minutes earlier.

The helicopter crew had to cut loose the ladder. Because the mountainous air was thin, a second chopper had a difficult time lifting off of the ridgeline, actually dragging the four-team members through the jungle before clearing the target area. A third chopper lifted out the three remaining Bru team members, carrying no more men due to weather and thin air conditions resulting from the height of the mountains. All three helicopters received heavy enemy ground fire.

As darkness closed in, CWO2 George P. Berg returned to the LZ to pick up the three remaining Green Berets. Helicopter crew chief Spec. 4 Walter Demsey and door gunner Gary L. Johnson lowered three STABO extraction harness rigs attached to ropes that were more than 100 feet long, to the trio of soldiers on the ground. (STABO harness rigs were designed by Special Forces during the war for extraction from the jungle when no landing zones were available. In the event a soldier was shot or knocked unconscious, the STABO rigs were designed to keep a soldier connected to the extraction rope.)

This is a 2015 photo of Cliff Newman on a hilltop near the Vietnam/Laotian border while working with DPAA recovery specialists to find the remains of RT Intruder members and the four 101st Airborne aviators who died in a horrific crash in 1971 while attempting to lift out team members while under intense, deadly enemy fire. (Photo Courtesy of Cliff Newman)

They hooked into the STABO rigs as Doc Watson gave the chopper crew the signal to lift out of the LZ. Berg began moving off of the LZ when NVA gunfire slammed into the aircraft. Demsey and Johnson returned furious gunfire from their M-60 machine guns. Hernandez was lifted to approximately 30-40 feet off the ground when his STABO rig snagged on a tree branch, snapping the rope that held him. The Green Beret fell to the ground, knocked unconscious.

He didn't hear NVA AAA fire slam into the Huey, literally knocking it out of the sky. The ill-fated helicopter traveled approximately 600 feet before it made an ugly U-turn and flipped over, crashing into the side of a granite-faced mountain, bursting into flames while also slamming Doc Watson and Baby Jesus Lloyd into the side of the cliff, killing them instantly.

Miraculously, Sammy Hernandez survived the fall. When he regained consciousness, he heard NVA soldiers and trackers searching for the men of RT Intruder. The stealthy jungle fighter moved silently into thick vegetation and hid for what would be a long night. When darkness fell, Hernandez emerged briefly from his hiding place, to slam his dislocated left shoulder into a tree in order to pop the shoulder bone back into the joint. Many years later, Hernandez simply said, "that really hurt. Believe me, I saw stars." With his shoulder sore, but no longer dislocated, Hernandez crawled back into his jungle hideaway.

The crash site of RT Intruder

On February 19, RT Habu, led by one-zero SSG Danzer, was inserted into the target to recover the dead bodies—presuming that Hernandez was KIA. Other Green Berets on that mission included Cliff Newman; SSG James Woodham, a medic; SFC Jimmy Horton; Sgt. Lemuel McGlothren; and SFC Charles Wesley, who had been lifted out of the target the previous day. Wesley volunteered for the mission and put one of the six body bags and extra ammo in his rucksack.

The expanded RT Habu was running a Bright Light mission— the most deadly of all SOG assignments because the NVA knew the

Green Berets, in coordination with air assets from the Air Force, Marine Corps, and Army, would be willing to die in an effort to recover Americans killed in action. When recon teams ran Bright Light missions, they carried no food, minimal water, extra ammo, hand grenades, body bags, bandages, and emergency medical supplies.

Shortly after RT Habu was inserted, a chase helicopter with Green Beret SGM Billy Waugh aboard spotted an American in an open area, flashing a bright-colored panel. It was Hernandez, who had crawled silently out of thicket to the open area and signaled the helicopter crew and Waugh. It picked up Hernandez and flew him back to Phu Bai.

Meanwhile, on the ground back at the target area, Covey—a Cessna O-2A, twin engine, light observation plane flown by Air Force 1st Lt. James (Woodstock) Hull with veteran recon man SFC Jose Fernandez flying in the right seat as Covey rider—located the crash site and directed RT Habu toward it, which was no easy task due to the thick jungle vegetation. For Fernandez, this was his second flight as a Covey rider after running recon for several years. Several times Hull flew the O-2A low, near tree-top level, to spot the team so Fernandez could provide it with accurate information as it moved through the thick jungle toward the crash site.

As they vectored the team to the end of the cliff several hundred feet above the crash site, the O-2A was hit with heavy enemy gunfire. It crashed a few miles away, killing both Hull and Fernandez, which added another layer of grief to a Bright Light mission attempting to recover six dead Americans.

Thanks to Hull and Fernandez though, RT Intruder located the crash site. They had to rappel down the cliff to reach the final resting spot of the destroyed helicopter and the six Americans. Eventually, the team placed the bodies of Berg, Woods, Johnson, and one leg— which they assumed was Demsey's, as the rest of Demsey's body couldn't be located – into body bags. These four body bags were stacked near the helicopter's frame to be lifted out by helicopter hoist in the morning.

Another grisly discovery was that of the bodies of Watson and Lloyd, hanging from trees on the cliff's face, still attached to their STABO rigs. Danzer determined that because night was falling, RT Habu should try to retrieve the bodies of the two recon men in the morning. The men of RT Habu hunkered into their RON for the night. They hoped that having the body bags next to the crash site, would improve the odds of being able to successfully remove them in the morning after retrieving the bodies of Watson and Lloyd.

However, in the morning, the NVA fiercely attacked RT Habu, wounding several team members. In order to survive, RT Habu reluctantly left behind the body bags, as it maneuvered away from the RON to get to a more advantageous position in the jungle to combat enemy troops while searching for an LZ and attending to wounded team members.

Meanwhile, a few miles away, Capt. Fred "Lightning" Wunderlich and three men from his recon team rappelled from a CH-53 helicopter onto the crashed O-2A. They confirmed that Hull and Fernandez were dead. That small Bright Light team recovered Fernandez' body from the wreckage, but team members couldn't recover Hull because the front engine of the O-2A had pinned him into the aircraft making it impossible to recover his body from it.

Across the A Shau Valley, Capt. Jim Butler and RT Python had been embroiled in intense combat with other NVA units, in fighting so intense that assistant team leader SSG Les Chapman fought hand-to-hand with NVA soldiers at one point during that team's battle. Butler had used Stinger and Spectre gunships, F-4 Phantom jets, A-1 Skyraiders, and numerous helicopter gunships from several helicopter units assigned to support SOG missions during that team's time on the ground. At one point, when team members from RT Habu and RT Python were fighting for their collective lives, Covey made radio contact with Butler, offering to pull RT Python out first due to the intense nature and the ferocity of the NVA attack on that team. Butler declined, he told Covey to pick up RT Habu first.

By the end of February 20th, an Air Force CH-53 pulled out RT Habu, flew the team—most of whom were wounded—back to a field hospital, then turned around and returned to the A Shau Valley to rescue RT Python, which suffered at least one KIA and several WIAs.

Still MIA

Today, those six Americans from RT Intruder and the four 101st Airborne aviators are among the 1,611 service members and civilians who are still listed as missing in action from the Vietnam War. They are among the more than 83,000 U.S. service members who remain missing in action today collectively from WWII, Korea, and Vietnam. People familiar with this overall POW/MIA mission concede that approximately 51,000 of those service members are listed as missing over deep ocean water—both Navy personnel and Air Force aviators, and will never be able to be recovered.

Under the new consolidation plan, DPAA brought three previous federal operations together under one command: the Defense POW/ Missing Personnel Office (DPMO), the Joint POW/MIA Accounting Command (JPAC), and the Air Force's Life Sciences Equipment Laboratory at Wright-Patterson Air Force Base in Ohio. On June 19, 2015 then-Secretary of Defense Ash Carter announced the Department of Defense Executive Service appointment of recently retired LTG Michael S. Linnington as director of the DPAA. However, he resigned in June 2016. One year later, that position remains unfilled in early June 2017.

Of special concern to Green Berets like Cliff Newman—who located the fallen Americans from RT Intruder 46 years ago but was unable to recover their bodies due to intense enemy gunfire—are the remains of 50 Green Berets and approximately 250 airmen who were lost in Laos during the eight-year secret war in Vietnam and are listed as missing in action, as the highly acidic soil of Southeast Asia attacks their remains.

In 2003, Newman, Wesley, and McGlothren returned to Southeast Asia to work with the Joint Task Force for Full Accounting in an attempt to locate the six Americans. That mission ended without locating them. Newman returned with a dedicated, hard-working

DPAA recovery team in June 2015. However, that effort, too, failed to pinpoint the location of the six Americans' remains because there was confusion about where the LZ should be cut for the DPAA team to use in 2015. As a result, where they landed was too far away to travel through dense Vietnam/Laotian jungle. However, he did praise the DPAA team he worked with in the field. "All I can say is, I'll gladly go back to help find them, that's the least I can do," Newman said. "However, I'm not getting any younger." That case number is 1706, and as of June 2017, there will be no DPAA in the field on that case until 2018.

One positive note: Hull's remains were recovered nine years ago and a formal burial service was held for him in Arlington National Cemetery in 2006.

PART III

This photo shows some of the equipment worn by ST Idaho members in the spring of 1969. Here, during an inspection by Lt. Gen. Richard Stilwell, the I Corps commander in S. Vietnam at that time, inspects the gear of Son, the ST Idaho point man for the special mission the team was preparing to run in Laos. Son, was dressed in NVA garb and equipment. Note his NVA vest across his chest, the AK-47 on his right hip and AK-47 magazines in his pouch. On far left, is John S. Meyer. On Meyer, note his Frank & Warren Survival Axe Type II, the radio wire connecting the handset in his jacket to the PRC-25 in his rucksack, his black contact gloves and sawed-off M-79 under his left arm.
(Photo Courtesy of John S. Meyer)

CHAPTER ELEVEN

Stuff We Carried/Stuff We Didn't Carry

Since Across The Fence was published in 2003, and because most of our missions with the Military Assistance Command Vietnam Studies and Observations Group (MACV-SOG) were classified top secret, I've received many inquiries about the equipment that I and fellow Special Forces soldiers carried when we ran reconnaissance missions into Laos, Cambodia and N. Vietnam and about the state-of-the-art weaponry, communications and surveillance equipment that we tested at the time—some of which we used in the field.

First, I turned to Lynne M. "Blackjack" Black Jr., to see what he carried as a conventional infantryman in South Vietnam with the 173rd Airborne Brigade during 1965 and 1966.

"When we went out on patrol the enemy could hear us coming a mile away," Black said. "The canteens were metal, with a metal chain that attached the black plastic cap to the body of the canteen. The metal canteen sat inside of a metal cup. As we walked that chain would bang on the canteen and the canteen sometimes rattled inside the metal cup. A squad of guys sounded like a Chinese drum line. Our weapon sling swivels would bang on the weapons providing even more noise. Dog tags would rattle as we walked." The paratroopers also wore metal helmets with the paratrooper

This is a photograph of a portion of a BAR harness, complete with pouches that held CAR-15 magazines.

This was the preferred harness by many SOG soldiers because its harness straps were padded and the pouches originally designed to hold magazines for the BAR (Browning Automatic Rifle) during World War II, held the small CAR-15 magazines and had a cover to protect the magazines from dirt, dust and rain. Additionally, there was enough room between some of the pouches where a canteen holder and plastic canteen could be held.

Note how the metal strap connectors are taped with black electric tape to reduce any glare and remove any metallic clicking sounds.

(Photo Courtesy of Alan R. Wise Collection)

chinstrap, with plastic helmet liners. Many paratroopers smoked and used Zippo lighters, which had a distinct, metallic clicking sound when opened and closed. They also wore jewelry such as silver or gold colored watches and rings, carried entrenching tools and L-shaped flashlights that attached to the upper web gear and often got caught in the brush. At night, if available, they would drink beer or soda from old tin cans that had to be opened with a can opener, as there were no pull-tabs on drinks at that time.

The infantrymen also carried: sleeping bags, gas masks, bayonets, personal knives, and rubber ponchos that were rolled and folded onto the back of the pistol belt. It provided a cushioned seat for sitting, but also a hiding place for small snakes, leeches, spiders and other jungle insects and creatures. Some paratroopers carried the claymore mine, with a hand generator, a PRC-25 radio, compass, maps and protractor. The basic ammo load for the M-16 or M-14 was 200 rounds plus hand grenades. Some wore heavy armored vests that absorbed water and were hot as hell, often quickly dehydrating the young soldiers.

The early paratroopers also wore their jump boots that Black called "fungus factories." Jungle boots, with canvas sides and a metal plate in the sole, were standard issue when I arrived in S. Vietnam in April 1968. The early paratroopers also wore military issued underwear that caused rashes and infections and socks that caused a foot fungus, a fungus some are still fighting today. It wasn't until a visit from the Secretary of State, who caught the fungus, that a cream was developed to fight it.

Nearly everyone smoked in those days. Five cigarettes were packed in neat little packs with each C-Ration meal. The smell of American cigarettes in Southeast Asia was unmistakable.

Louis J. DeSeta also served with the 173rd in 1967 before he volunteered for SOG duty. "We were noisy as hell in the 173rd," he said. "We used to carry those metal ammo boxes that always banged against the metal canteens. Even taking a drink of water with the metal canteen made a metallic noise that could be heard off in the distance. A lot of us carried a poncho, but often didn't use it in the field because they were so noisy when you unfolded them. And, once it started to rain, the rain hitting them gave off a different noise that the enemy could hear.

"SOG was just the total, complete opposite. We carried nothing that made any noise. Everything was taped down or tied down."

DeSeta and Black agreed that the men who served in the early phases of the war had to learn what not to do and to pass along their lessons learned to the FNG's.

Stuff We Didn't Carry

To avoid rashes, infections and fungus, Black and I didn't wear underwear or socks. All SOG recon men didn't wear helmets, helmet liners or armored vests of any sort. Most of us didn't carry entrenching tools, bayonets, sleeping bags, hammocks, ponchos, ponchos liners or air mattresses because they added weight to our total load. I weighed my gear on a small scale once at Phu Bai and it weighed approximately 90 pounds. No one carried an M-16, an M-14 or a 9 mm weapon as his primary weapon.

For all missions we never carried any form of identification: no dog tags, no military ID cards, no letters from home—nothing with any personal information on it. Our uniforms were sterile: no rank, no unit designator, no jump wings, no CIB or South Vietnamese jump wings were displayed. Our green beret remained at FOB 1. We went to extreme measures to insure that our anonymity remained in tact to provide deniability to the U.S. government in the event we were killed or captured. We cut out the section of a target map to carry to the field, thus only showing the grid in the target area, with no further information about the map or the cartographers who produced them. Additionally, we never smoked or cooked in the field.

Stuff We Carried

The most important piece of equipment we carried was the CAR-15. The sling for it would vary: sometimes I used a cravat or a canvas strap taped tightly to both ends of the weapon for soundless movements. That was the preferred weapon of choice by everyone on ST Idaho. The only exception was an AK-47 for Son when he was our point man wearing an NVA uniform, and an M-79 carried by our grenadier. In November 1968, Henry King carried the experimental pump M-79 weapon on one mission. It held up to five rounds of 40 mm high explosive ammunition. His secondary weapon was the Model 1911 Colt .45. On occasions, Black would carry the M-60 machine gun.

Every American on ST Idaho carried a sawed-off M-79 for additional firepower. We thought of it as our hand-held artillery. During patrol, the Americans would load a special M-79 round with fleshettes or double-ought (00) buckshot for close contact. The sawed-off M-79 would be secured either with a canvas or rope lanyard or a D-ring that was covered with black electrical tape to prevent any metallic banging. During the fall of 1968, I had a one-of-a-kind sawed-off M-79 holster, which I lost in when I was unconscious after a rope extraction in Laos.

I would carry at least thirty-four 20-round magazines for the CAR-15—we only placed 18 rounds in each magazine, which gave me 612 rounds for that weapon, and at least 12 rounds for the M-79. The CAR-15 magazines were placed in ammo pouches or cloth canteen pouches, with the bottoms facing up to prevent debris from getting into the magazine and all of the rounds pointing away from the body. We taped black electrical tape to the bottom of each magazine to make it easier to grab them out of the pouch during firefights. I also carried 10 to 12 fragmentation grenades, a few of the older M-26, the newer M-33 "baseball" grenades and one or two V-22 minigrenades.

For headgear, I only wore a green cravat, a triangular bandage, on missions. It was light, didn't get caught on jungle branches, or knocked off my head by prop wash and it broke up the color of my blond hair. As a practical matter, it kept the sweat out of my eyes—hats didn't do that. I often wore camouflage "paint" on my face.

I wore the traditional Army jungle fatigues because they dried quicker while on the ground than the camouflage fatigues available at the time. I had the Phu Bai tailor sew an extra zipped pocket on

Among the weapons carried by SOG recon teams included, from the top:

First row: a CAR-15, with 20-round magazine and weapon sling.

Second row: a traditional 40 mm M-79 grenade launcher.

Third row: from left, an M-79 ammo pouch that holds three rounds, a 40 mm tear gas round and a high-explosive round (gold-colored tip) for the M-79, a sawed-off M-79 with rappelling D-ring in the trigger guard.

Bottom row: from left' a claymore mine with connector wire and detonator; a Browning Hi Power 9 mm semiautomatic pistol and a mini-grenade.

Photo Courtesy of Alan R. Wise Collection

the upper right and left arm (see cover of book) where I carried pens, notebooks, pen flares, one plastic spoon and my signal mirror. The tailor also sewed zipped pockets between the front top and bottom buttoned pockets, where I'd place maps, morphine syrettes, an extra notebook with any mission specific notes and the URC-10 emergency radio.

On my right wrist I wore a black, self-winding, luminescent Seiko watch, which was so bright at night that I wore it face down on the bottom of my wrist, under my glove. Thus, even in the pitch-black jungle, I knew when to make communication checks with the airborne command aircraft, usually at midnight, or at 2 a.m. In the jungle I always wore black contact gloves for protection against jungle plants, thorns and insects. I cut the thumb, index finger and middle finger off of the right glove down to the first joint, for improved grip. I always wore an extra cravat around my neck.

On my left harness strap, I taped my K-Bar knife, with handle facing down, hand grenades, small smoke canisters and a sterile bandage. On my right harness strap was a strobe light, held in a cloth pouch, hand grenades, a rappelling D-ring, and a smoke grenade. My preferred web gear was the WW II BAR (Browning Automatic Rifle) ammo belt and shoulder straps because five CAR-15 magazines fit snugly into each individual pouch. One pouch would be used for M-79 rounds. A plastic water canteen in a cloth canteen holder would be fit onto the belt, as well as one white phosphorous grenade and my survival ax.

The amount of water available in the AO would determine how many plastic canteens of water I'd carry to the field. One canteen would have a small bottle of water purification pills taped to it. I used those pills for all water outside of camp. The water in our AO's was often tainted with the defoliant Agent Orange—we hoped the purification tablets would counteract it. On the right side of my harness I always carried the Frank & Warren Survival Ax Type II, MIL-S-8642C. I preferred it to the machete because the backside had a nasty sharp hook that cut through jungle vines on the return swing. I carried my folding compass around my neck, held by green parachute cord.

I used a cravat as a belt, because it was silent. In my right pocket was the Swiss Army knife, secured by a green parachute cord to a belt loop on my pants. Because I always wore the bulky gas mask bag on my left side, which held the black M-17 gas mask, I rarely put anything in my upper left pocket. (If the charcoal air filters on the M-17 got wet they had to be replaced.) In my lower left pant pocket I carried a small and large colored panels to mark our position for Covey and tactical air strikes. In my lower right pocket were extra pen flares, a dehydrated Long-Range Reconnaissance Patrol ration (LRRP, pronounced LURP), bug repellant to squirt on leeches and an extra cravat and sterile bandage. I always carried the Swiss rope. The 12-foot section of green-colored rope was used for a Swiss seat for extractions by helicopter. We would hook a D-ring through the seat's rope and onto 150-foot-long pieces of rope that hung from the chopper.

On all missions, I carried the PRC-25, our primary radio contact with the outside world. It took up the most space in my indig rucksack. Most times I had the short, flexible antenna screwed into it, which was folded under my right arm and tucked into my jungle fatigue jacket because the NVA always searched for the radio operator, knowing he was the primary link to U.S. air power. I carried the long antenna, folded in sections, in my rucksack.

Other items included: one can of C-Ration fresh fruit, either peaches or apricots, extra hand grenades, the remainder of my CAR-15 magazines, extra M-79 rounds—including one tear-gas round, an Army long-sleeved sweater, a thin, hooded waist-length plastic rain jacket and toilet paper. Both the sweater and rain jacket would be folded under the PRC-25 to buffer where it hit my back. I also carried an extra PRC-25 battery, an extra URC-10 battery, extra smoke grenades, an extra canteen of water if needed, and extra LRRPs.

On a few occasions, especially when we ran targets in Cambodia, which was flatter and more wide open, I'd carry a claymore mine and a few pre-cut fuses: five-second, 10-second and longer-duration fuses, used to break contact with enemy troops chasing us. On several occasions I carried .22-caliber High Standard semi-automatic pistol with a silencer for ambushes or to kill enemy tracker dogs. I also carried cough syrup for Hiep or anyone who coughed at night, cans of black pepper and powdered mace for enemy tracker dogs and a compact toothbrush.

There are some redundancies, such as bullets, bandages and smoke grenades carried in various locations on my body because each could be crucial to surviving a firefight and successfully directing helicopter gun ships, F-4 Phantom jets that delivered ordnance on target faster than the speed of sound and the old deadly propeller-driven A-1E Skyraiders.

The emphasis was packing firepower for survival. I preferred to go hungry as to running out of ammo. Items for creature comfort were discarded in favor of carrying an extra grenade or a high-explosive M-79 round. Why?

In the Prairie Fire AO there were several times when we were in contact with NVA troops for two or three hours before making radio contact with Covey or any U.S. aircraft. Then, depending on weather and the status of other teams in the field, there would be further delays in getting air assets on scene, especially when the team was surrounded and there were no routes for escape and evasion. On most missions, I preferred six-man teams due to helicopter extraction considerations: height, altitude, weight and weather conditions dictated how many men could board an extraction chopper. The type of helicopter used for the extraction could vary from the old H-34, to Hueys, or on rare occasions, the Air Force's HH-3 Jolly Green Giant, the larger, more powerful chopper during that war. Which one picked up the team, usually under heavy enemy gunfire, made a difference in how many men it could carry in extreme weather conditions.

There were at least two missions when ST Idaho was extracted from the target, I was down to my last CAR-15 magazine, M-26 grenade and M-79 round. The NVA was relentless and fearless.

We had an intimate knowledge of all the weapons we carried to the field. Not only did we know how they worked but we could dismantle them and clean them at night—that was mandatory

Other equipment SOG teams carried included, from the upper left:

First row: Pentax single-lens reflex camera; signal mirror; Air Force pen light; strobe light and smoke canisters.

Second row: a mini-grenade; a hand-held, single-shot pen flare launcher and flares; and an URC-10 ultra-high frequency emergency radio.

Bottom row: one-pound of C-4 plastic explosive and a box of blasting caps.

Photo Courtesy of Alan R. Wise Collection

training, not optional. We fired thousands of rounds through our CAR-15s and M-79s during live-fire reaction drills and firing at static targets. Before we carried any new weapon or device to the field on a mission we practiced using them for hours in order to gain familiarity with them and to see how they functioned under repetitive conditions. With ST Idaho, if the team wasn't on a mission we were training on the range or doing local training patrols, which included both silent and live-fire reaction drills.

For wiretaps, Sau was the quickest team member to climb an NVA telephone pole or tree to install a wiretap. He trained several other men on the team, including Phouc, Hung, Quang and Son. They had to climb the pole, install the wiretap and cover the wire leading from the telephone wire down to our cassette tape recorder with mud or wood putty, to hide it from passing enemy troops.

For Bright Light missions, we carried extra rounds, hand grenades, claymore mines, bandages and medical supplies, and at least one machine gun. We carried one canteen of water, no food.

On a few missions we carried antitank and antivehicular mines. Before going to the field, Black or Shore would spend hours cross training our Vietnamese team members to insure installing the devices as quickly as possible without detection by enemy troops while the remainder of the team provided security for them. On those missions we'd usually carry at least one M-72 Light Antitank Weapon (LAW), but only after the entire team had drilled on them for several days.

For POW snatches, ST Idaho spent hours practicing setting up the jungle ambush. This entailed each team member quickly placing a claymore mine in the kill zone and for flank security, in addition to installing the pre-cut block of plastic explosive that would knock out an enemy soldier. The claymore mine, officially designated the M-18A1 fragmentation, antipersonnel mine, weighed 3.5 pounds and contained 1.5 pounds of plastic explosive which propelled 700 steel balls in a deadly, killing arc that was dangerous out to 250 meters.

During the course of 1968 there were experimental weapons that S-4 shared with recon men for our assessment of their performance capabilities, such as the Gyrojet rocket pistol that fired a 13 mm round similar in gauge but longer than the standard .45 caliber round. There were many variations of silenced weapons such as the M-1 carbine, the old WW II Sten submachine gun, the 9 mm Karl Gustav Swedish K submachine gun, the XM-21 sniper rifle, various night-vision devices and the experimental pump M-79 weapon. The Air Force and the CIA often came to us with experimental explosive devices, communications equipment and various trail sensors. Later, in the early 70s, the Air Force used recon team experiences combating the NVA at night to design complicated enemy-targeting devices, some of which lead to technology used in the wars in Iraq and Afghanistan following the terrorists attacks on the Twin Towers in New York City on Sept. 11, 2001.

Sometimes team members were issued devices that were unknown to me. For example, in 2005 Doug LeTourneau told me about a team perimeter security device that he carried with him on all missions. It was a small box that held a small strand of nylon filament he placed around the team's perimeter. He would place the listening device near his ear. If a person or an animal walked through the team's perimeter, it would sound a barely audible alert signal. For a short period of time, Black used a seismic alert system made up of four probes, each emitting its own signal. He had a receiver in his breast pocket with an ear jack that allowed him to hear the warning signals from each probe. Unfortunately, if it was used in heavy grassed areas any wind moving the grass would set off the probes, falsely indicating the team was surrounded. Once we discovered this flaw in the system it was abandoned. Not all technology worked out.

Lastly, LeTourneau also reminded me that he took "no-shit" pills before a mission, which prevented bowel movements. I didn't use them. Enough said on that topic.

Editor's note: *To see instructions on tying a Swiss seat, go to:* http://www.youtube.com/watch?v=ssmYruwGTzM

CHAPTER TWELVE

He Supplied/Invented the Stuff SOG Carried

One of the deepest, best-kept secrets during SOG's eight-year secret war was who supplied the Green Berets – both those running top secret missions across the fence and those assigned to tradition Special Forces A Camps – with everything from new highly-specialized equipment and weapons to indigenous rations.

As the OSS had unique, top-secret supply channels during World War II, so did the Green Berets in Southeast Asia. Few knew where OSS agents and Jedburgh teams obtained those supplies during WW II, and the same was true in Vietnam for the Green Berets.

When Special Forces soldiers in Southeast Asia needed specialized supplies, they turned to Counterinsurgency Support Office (CISO), where Deputy Commander Conrad Bennet ("Ben") Baker worked in quiet obscurity in Okinawa, far from any public or enemy scrutiny. Many never knew his name or the acronym CISO. Regardless, Baker didn't sit on his ass all day dreaming up stuff to send to the troops; he traveled to Southeast Asia more than 80 times to meet the warriors he served, to speak to the Green Berets in the field and to their "little people," the indigenous troops who fought side by side with them against the communists.

It all had a quiet, very private beginning in June 1963 when

This photo of Conrad Bennet "Ben" Baker was taken in the early 60s during one of his visits to Southeast Asia, standing here with a young, indigenous soldier. (Photo Courtesy of Conrad Bennet "Ben" Baker)

Baker was appointed as deputy chief of the newly formed CISO office. Baker said, "It was a highly classified unit tasked with the logistical support of Special Forces paramilitary training and all SOG missions. Don't forget, we also conducted limited research and development for SF and the agency. We, or CISO I should say and the amazing CISO staff, took over responsibilities from the CIA under the Parasol-Switchback Program (in 1963), where the Army gained complete control over such operations. When SOG was activated in 1964, there was a critical need for non-attributable (sterile) equipment.... We had women working 24 hours a day back in Okinawa in order to respond in a quick, appropriate fashion. It was hectic, I can tell you that, but we did it. Early on, they needed Special Forces machetes; within 90 days we placed our first order for 15,000 and had them delivered to SF men....

"SOG was the highest support priority of any unit in the world at that time. We had what we called the Quick Reacting Procurement (QRP) system to expedite our acquisitions. Those (SOG) missions were going across the fence and if captured or killed, our country needed plausible deniability for those heroic Green Berets, because officially our government's position stated that we had no troops stationed in N. Vietnam, Laos or Cambodia." Thus, he said, SOG fell under CISO's wing for out-of-country support.

"In the early days," Baker said, "SF needed everything. You name it, from uniforms that fit men four to five feet tall, who wore small size three extra-wide jungle boots, to medicines for rare but deadly jungle-related diseases and infections."

As more Green Berets began serving in Vietnam and in the secret war, they often submitted unique, specific supply requests to CISO, for items that weren't available in routine military supply channels: New items at the time were cassette tape recorders that were used to wiretap NVA phone lines; Olympus 35-mm Pen EE cameras; the first night vision equipment – including the early Starlight Scope, which was heavy and ruined the night vision of the operator but enabled soldiers in an ambush to distinguish between armed-enemy troops and civilians; NVA copycat uniforms, rucksacks, and boots worn by SOG team members; and leggings to prevent leeches from crawling up soldiers' legs.

"Because of the clandestine nature of the secret war, CISO and SOG had top priority for anything from air conditioners to SOG knives to weapons," said Baker, during a May 21 telephone interview. "Sometimes we'd piss off people, like the Marines, for example. We had a situation where some of the (Special Forces) A Camps down south in IV Corps needed air conditioners for their commo sheds. We requisitioned them from the Marines for those teams. Believe me, they weren't happy, but SF had top priority."

Former OSS agent (Ret) Maj. Gen. John K. Singlaub, who served two years as Chief SOG – the officer in charge of SOG from May 14, 1966 to Aug. 2 1968 – described Baker as the critical, behind-the-scenes player in SOG's secret war. "He was a supply wizard," Singlaub said in an April 2017 interview conducted in Tennessee. "Whether we needed High Standard 22s with silencers or special equipment for our indigenous soldiers, Ben would get it for us, one way or the other."

Retired Green Beret Lt. Col. Gene McCarley, who ran SOG top secret recon missions out of FOB 2 in Kontum – including a September 1970 raid that was one of the most successful SOG Hatchet Force missions deep into Laos – knew Baker and marveled at his prowess in obtaining critical supplies and weapons. "I had the honor of meeting Ben a few times. He wouldn't remember me, but I can say that he provided us with a lot of things that we needed that weren't available through routine supply channels. He cared about the troops. If we needed things he'd find them. If things weren't available, he'd invent them."

Baker said, "We did a lot of little things to help the men of SOG and other agencies. For example, in the early days of the war, SF used the HT-1 radio, but those radios used BA-30 batteries, the old lead-acid battery that was highly inefficient. We changed to alkaline batteries and we purchased the best, which were made in Japan at that time. We had no 'must buy American' mandates. Our job was to get the best supplies needed for our troops, plain and simple."

Within SOG annals, Baker earned his legendary status for many reasons, including his unique inventions and the items he purchased and/or helped to refine, which included:

- Inventing indigenous rations: "Early in the war," Baker said, "the Montagnards were getting the runs from U.S. rations. So I went over to Nam and Laos, talked to some key nutritionists there and put together indigenous rations, which consisted of precooked rice placed in a plastic bag shaped like a tube. The rice I laced with Vitamin B because the 'Yards had a vitamin deficiency." Baker went to Taiwan, got pre-cooked rice, then developed several rice seasonings – beef, fish, squid and mutton, to name a few. When he went to United States Army Natick Soldier Research, Development and Engineering Center (NSR-DEC) to get that sort of specific ration, "they told me it would take two to three years to produce it. That's nuts," Baker said. He went to a private company, placed an order for 30,000 meals for "about a buck a piece," and sent the bill up the chain of command. By the end of the Vietnam War, Baker estimates that CISO had sent at least 66 million individual indigenous rations that were used by U.S. allies in Vietnam, Laos, Thailand and other locations. Highly respected 5th Special Forces Group Commander Col. Robert Rheault "estimated that we may have used more than 80 million.... I'm not going to argue with the colonel," Baker said.
- Inventing "Eldest Son" ammo that exploded when used by enemy troops in their AK-47 or 82 mm mortar, killing or maiming the enemy. "Also, we had old PRC-10 radios," said Baker. "Instead

Conrad Bennet "Ben" Baker, center, holds two versions of the famous SOG knives that he invented while serving as the deputy director of CISO during the Vietnam War. Standing with Baker are, left SGM (ret.) Ron Courtney and SGM (ret.) Ernie Jensen, both Green Berets served in Vietnam.
(Photo Courtesy of George Eleopoulos, SFA Chap. 23)

of getting rid of them, we packed them with C-4 and would leave the battery in it and drop it in enemy territory. When an enemy would squeeze the talk key, it would explode."

- Inventing the first SOG Knife: "The first model of it, I used a spring from a Jeep, due to its metallic strength. However, I didn't like it and threw it into the ocean," Baker said. "I used the stacked leather handle on it; that was an idea I got from my father's Marbles Gladstone Skinning Knife.... My design of the first seven-inch SOG Knife had a tilt upward edge to the blade for maximum penetration. The fighting was close-quarter and vicious.... It probably was the rarest production knife used by our troops in Southeast Asia. I designed it so the weight and balance made it a good throwing knife too. I believe (Green Beret Medal of Honor Recipient SGM) Jon Cavaiani told me he threw the knife at an NVA soldier and it killed him." The first order of 1,300 SOG Knives went to Yogi Shokai, the Japanese trading company CISO worked with at that time. "That order went out on June 6, 1964, exactly 20 years after D-Day. I'll never forget that date," Baker said.

- Indig Rucks: "We invented the Indig Rucks because the things the CIA were using at that time were too big for the indigenous troops working with SF and the agency," Baker said. All SOG teams used those rucks throughout the war.

- Improved jungle boots: "(At CISO) We tried to think ahead, we took trips to Southeast Asia to talk to the men in the field. We believed that it should be the man in the field who should determine what their troops need, not some fat-assed bureaucrat sitting behind some a desk at DoD or the White House. When they came out with jungle boots we put the metal plate in the bottom due to the gosh-awful punji sticks the SF men and their indig were encountering in 'Nam – sharpened sticks that had been dipped in human excrement to worsen the infection."

Baker made more than 80 visits to Southeast Asia during the Vietnam War. "Sometimes, it was the little things that counted," Baker said. "If they needed socks, we'd send them bundles of socks. If they needed black berets, we got them. When they asked for black rain gear that wasn't too long, we got it for them." Today, those blacks pullover SOG rain jackets are collectors items valued at hundreds of dollars.

And, there was a practical side to Baker too: "At one point, every team wanted 12 or 13 Rolex watches, the Oyster model I believe. They got Seiko watches instead that cost $6 or $8 apiece." The Seiko watches were among the first self-winding watches that any paratroopers had seen, complete with luminous dials, and displaying the day and date. The luminous dial was so bright SOG recon men had to cover it with gloves or black electric tape at night. Baker was quick to point out how he saved approximately $170,000 over 10 years when purchasing more than 32,000 machetes by having them made in Japan at a cost of $2 plus, compared to U.S. company estimates of $8 plus per machete. "I always tried to save a penny when possible," he added.

Also, there were times that Baker or his staff would send experimental weapons to SOG recon teams for testing and opinions. For example, during 1968 at the top secret SOG base, FOB 1 in Phu Bai, CISO staff sent a Gyrojet rocket pistol that fired a 13 mm round and a large pump shotgun that fired the 40 mm round used in the M-79 grenade launcher. The gyro pistol was turned back, and the experimental pump was turned back after ST Idaho carried it on one mission. It had a bad habit of jamming while extracting the empty cartridge. When it worked, five rounds could be fired in less than a minute, which gave a six-man recon team a lot of firepower, but a lot of extra weight to carry in the field.

Last, but not least, "My name is on that damned Bolo Machete," Baker said, spitting the words out of his mouth. "That's a hunk of shit. Some damned general somewhere ordered someone to make it, they did, and because I put the wooden handle on it, my name is on it. That's one I'm not proud of…. We went out and got better stuff like the Survival Ax Type (produced by Frank and Warren Inc.)."

Baker Honored by SF Regiment

Because of his dedication and due diligence over the years, Baker was formally inducted into the Special Forces Regiment as the 12th Honorary Member on April 27, 2017 by Colonel Nestor A. Sadler, Commandant of the U.S. Army John F. Kennedy Special Warfare Center and School.

After World War II, Baker served briefly in General Douglas MacArthur's headquarters staff in 1947 before putting his organization and logistics skills to work with Field Engineers. In 1963, as a civilian, he was working in Okinawa when Special Forces Capt. David E. Watts put together CISO, with Baker leading the development of the new office. CISO supplied clothing, weapons and equipment to Special Forces, some federal agencies and to indigenous forces operating in Vietnam and denied areas. Baker served as deputy CISO commander from June 1963 to October 1972 where he traveled up and down and the width and breadth of Vietnam. His travels included more than 80 trips to forward base camps in Vietnam while providing Special Forces Soldiers and Vietnamese allies with support not available through normal channels.

He conducted many of those missions with Special Forces Legend Walter L. Shumate, who was a Sergeant First Class at that time, later retiring as a Sgt. Major. Baker was instrumental in organizing and executing classified trips with Shumate that had a significant, positive influence on the Special Forces mission, including providing unique and experimental weapons tested by

Conrad Bennet "Ben" Baker was inducted as the 12th Honorary Member of the Special Forces Regiment on April 27, 2017 in Northern California. Amongst the many achievements Baker accomplished as the deputy director for the Counter-insurgency Support Office that served SOG, Special Forces and other agencies during the Vietnam War was the research and development of specially designed rations for the indigenous troops who support Special Forces and other agencies during the Vietnam War. Under Project PIR, Baker is seen holding a box of In-digenous Rations used by Montagnards other indigenous personnel during the war. Baker estimated that 66 to 86 million Indigenous Rations were purchased and provided to troops supporting the U.S. war effort. (Photo Courtesy of George Eleopoulos, SFA Chap. 23)

SOG Recon Teams and other top secret operations.

When Baker's name was mentioned to living spec ops legend, (Ret) Maj. Gen. John K. Singlaub, the legendary OSS agent pulled out his official two-star, major-general stationery, and wrote a congratulatory note to Baker, which author John Stryker Meyer read aloud during a luncheon honoring Baker on April 27 at the Basque Cultural Center, in South San Francisco. Singlaub's doctors wouldn't let him fly at that time.

Singlaub's note to Baker read:

"Dear Ben, I just want to add my feelings to your recent honor and to thank you for spending so many years providing your special skills and ideas to the whole Special Operations Community in the Western Pacific. We all benefitted from your activities and years of service.

"Please accept my most sincere thanks and congratulations. John K. Singlaub, Maj Gen, USA (Ret)."

Baker's face broke into a large smile when he received Singlaub's note. "He remembered me? That's amazing," he said, as he read the note out loud to his wife Shirley and members of the Special Forces Association and Special Operations Association.

In recent months, there have been media reports about ammunition that explodes when used by enemy troops. With a sparkle in his eye while reflecting on his Vietnam War creation of "Eldest Son" enemy ordnance, Baker said, "We had an impact on the enemy's psyche then and I'm glad to see it's still happening today."

On Feb. 13, 1971, Brigadier Gen. Michael D. Healy awarded Baker an honorary Green Beret for his due diligence and creative efforts during his tenure at CISO. He was also awarded the Meritorious Service Medal for civilians on Dec. 17, 1974.

Conrad Bennet "Ben" Baker stands behind the formal induction certification into the U.S. Army Special Forces Regiment, the highest honor bestowed upon civilians by the regiment. Baker is the 12th recipient of the HMOR. From left, MSG David Nolan; Mrs. Shirley Baker; Baker; and Col. Nestor A. Sadler, Special Forces Regimental Commandant U.S. Army John F. Kennedy Special Warfare Center and School at Ft. Bragg. NC. Sadler presided over the formal induction of Baker into the Regiment. (Photo Courtesy of George Eleopoulous, SFA Chap. 23)

Dear Ben,
    I just want to add my feelings to your
recent honor and to thank you for spending
so many years providing your special skills
and ideas to the whole Special Operations
Community in the western Pacific. We all
benefited from your activities and years of
service.
    Please accept my most sincere thanks
and congratulations.
                        John K. Singlaub
                        Maj Gen, USA (Ret)

On April 27, 2017 Conrad Bennet "Ben" Baker was formally inducted into the
U.S. Army Special Forces Regiment as only the 12th Honorary Members by Col.
Nestor A. Sadler, commandant of the U.S. Army John F. Kennedy Special Warfare
Center and School. On that day, a hand-written note to Baker from living spec ops
legend (Ret.) Maj. Gen. John K. Singlaub, the legendary OSS agent during World
War II and was Chief SOG, from 1966-68 — the commander of SOG operations.
Singlaub said Baker was a "supply wizard" and a SOG legend in his own right.

On March 12, 2017, SPAD pilot and commander officer of OLAA A1 Skyraiders that flew in support of Operation Tailwind from Sept. 11-14, Mel Swanson died at age 84. A celebration of life for Mel Swanson was held April 21-23 at the Tennessee Museum of Aviation in Sevierville, TN. Here, former SOG members, SPAD pilots and museum staff joined for a final salute as Museum Founder Neal Melton takes off in the A1-H Skyraider, Tail Number 665, to perform a ceremonial spreading of Swanson's ashes. (Photo Courtesy of Chuck Kasbeer)

EPILOGUE

"A reputation once broken may possibly be repaired, but the world will always keep their eyes on the spot where the crack was." —Joseph Hall

There's a dark, unforgiving, ruinous side of the Internet that can wreck or taint a man's reputation forever with the click of a send button.

Equally as dangerous is the destructive power of television, especially when a once-respected cable news network advertises a "news special" for days before it broadcasts a fabricated, false story that erroneously portrays heroic Green Berets as war criminals – a portrayal/betrayal of truth that many of those Special Forces soldiers and their families watched live in shock and utter horror in 1998. A news magazine printed a version of the fake news story, increasing their collective agony.

Adding to the pain and ignominy of being portrayed as war criminals, network reporters/editors first interviewed many of the Green Berets who participated in Operation Tailwind by saying they were going to broadcast a story about the uniqueness of the mission and the valor of the men on the ground, as well as the Army, Air Force and Marine Corps aviators who put their lives on the line supporting them. After 28 years of avowed silence, many Operation Tailwind

183

Tennessee Museum of Aviation Founder/Pilot Neal Melton climbs down from the museum's A1-H Skyraider after the ceremonial dumping of Mel Swanson's ashes from the aircraft on April 22, 2017. (Photo Courtesy of Mel Swanson's Family)

participants thought it would be OK to have a story detailing the valor of that mission.

I was an editor at a local newspaper in Oceanside, CA at the time. I never saw the original CNN broadcast nor read the Time magazine echo-story where reporters falsely alleged that Operation Tailwind Green Berets went into Laos to kill American military POWs and defectors who had left the battlefields of S. Vietnam for the sanctuary of Laos. And, the reporters said American aviators dropped deadly Sarin nerve gas on those American dissidents as well as "innocent" women and children. At that time, my wife and I had four teenagers and a one-year-old at home and our newspaper was locked in a competitive newspaper war in N. San Diego County. I didn't have a local angle to write about the fabrication, thus it stayed on my journalist's back burner. By the time the CNN story and repetitive Time magazine piece were proven wrong by a DoD investigation and an internal committee headed by respected media attorney Floyd Abrams, I wanted to write about the travesty but was told that some of the men shown on screen were obtaining attorneys and didn't want to talk about it for the record.

I waited, while staying busy at work, home and, with the encouragement of my wife Anna, began interviewing for my first non-fiction SOG book, *Across The Fence, The Secret War in Vietnam*. In 2004, there was a meeting between attorneys and some of the men from Operation Tailwind to discuss attempts to put together a documentary officially correcting for the record the CNN fake news take on Operation Tailwind. It never came to fruition. Highly-acclaimed Houston attorney Jim Moriarty said CNN had initially promised to broadcast a follow-up piece, but it never materialized.

Over the years, I attempted to write about it, but the pieces never came together until 2014, after the SOA Reunion in Las Vegas where I finally met a few of the A-1 Skyraider pilots who supported Operation Tailwind. SOFREP.com editor Jack Murphy gave me the green light to write a multi-part series for that online website. After several months of interviews, research and meetings with Moriarty – a Marine Corps door gunner who spent three tours of duty in Vietnam

– the pieces came together in a six-part SOFREP.com series on Operation Tailwind. By this time Moriarty had supported the men of Operation Tailwind spiritually and within the legal system for more than a decade, outraged at the bold-faced lies CNN broadcast and Time magazine printed in 1998. I also had assistance from resource/analyst extraordinaire Ellen Cousins and A-1 Skyraider pilots Mel Swanson and Don Engebretsen, Green Berets Gene McCarley and Gary Mike Rose, Scarface pilots Joe Driscoll and Barry Pencek, and Dimmer studs Don Persky and Larry Groah. I focused strictly on the valor of the mission and didn't write about CNN's journalistic prevarications. After CNN was called out publicly in 2017 with new allegations of broadcasting fake news, I wrote a piece for SOFREP.com on its 1998 embarrassing fake news and the harm it brought to the men of Operation Tailwind.

During and after the April 2016 Operation Tailwind reunion at the Tennessee Museum of Aviation History several operators, including Air Force Lt. Col. Mel Swanson, and a few others asked me to write a book about those four historic days in Laos from Sept. 11, 1970 to Sept. 14, 1970.

Because there are so many SOG mission stories that remain untold, my wife and a few close friends liked the idea of starting a SOG series of books, with SOG Chronicles Volume One featuring Operation Tailwind as the centerpiece – putting it in a book 47 years after CCC B Company Hatchet Force of 16 Green Berets and 120 indigenous personnel successfully accomplished the suicide mission: Take the pressure off of the 5,000-man CIA operation in southern Laos. And, the men of Company B – under the savvy, fearless leadership of then-Capt. Gene McCarley – pulled off one of the most successful intelligence coups of the secret war with the capture of critical, insightful enemy documents from an enemy battalion headquarters the Green Berets overran and later destroyed. A quote from Oliver Wendell Holmes, Sr. captured McCarley's leadership skill set on that mission: *"Have the courage to act, instead of react."*

And finally, I got to meet some of the additional men who were on the ground during that mission: McCarley, Bernie Bright, Mike Hagen and the modest Green Beret medic Gary "Just call me Mike" Rose, and his remarkable wife Margaret.

Today, if anyone ran into any of the Green Berets, A-1 Skyraider, Cobra gunship or Dimmer pilots/crew members, they'd appear outwardly to be just another gray-haired man walking down the street. But, they accomplished great deeds, performed to the highest standards of military conduct against an ever-increasingly violent, unforgiving and well-armed communist enemy. America needs to be aware of their incredible story. After the war, those men, as millions of Americans before them had from the days of the Revolutionary War, WW II and Korean War, put down their weapons, put away their uniforms and returned to the streets of America and productive lives – a scene replayed by hundreds and thousands of veterans from those many wars yesterday and the 16-year-long wars today, in 2017.

And, last but not least the secret war, including Operation Tailwind in particular, set the stage for today's special operations, first demonstrating how Army, Air Force and Marine Corps aviation units could work together with amazingly accurate Close Air Support of elite Green Beret soldiers on a secret mission far behind enemy lines. (Tragically, some of those lessons were either ignored or forgotten in 1979 during Operation Eagle Claw, the fateful mission to rescue the 52 hostages held in Tehran, Iran.)

During the eight-year secret war in Vietnam, Laos and Cambodia, SOG soldiers pioneered:

- Helicopter insertion/extraction techniques, including the first rope exfiltrations from the jungle where helicopters couldn't land due to thick triple-canopy jungle. SOG had the first HALO (High Altitude, Low Opening) combat parachute jumps into Laos. There were several HALO jumps, and later teams performed traditional combat jumps into Laos.
- Developing and improving ground-to-air communications and techniques for land navigation and direction of Close Air Support assets.

After Museum Founder and Pilot Neal Melton returned from a ceremonial flight with Mel Swanson's ashes, several SPAD pilots who served with Swanson in Vietnam signed an autograph under the air brake of A1-H Skyraider Tail Number 665. Here, Swanson's daughter Frances Kaklikian signs a note to her father. (Photo Courtesy of SOG Chronicles Publishing)

This is the loving note Swanson's daughter Frances Kaklikian wrote under the air brake of A1-H Skyraider Tail Number 665.
(Photo Courtesy of SOG Chronicles Publishing)

- Wire-tapping techniques and sophisticated ambush/ POW snatch techniques.
- Leaving rigged communist ammunition in enemy territory that would explode in the face of enemy soldiers, usually killing them while having the psychological impact of enemy troops doubting the reliability of their munitions.
- And, SOG soldiers carried the Colt CAR-15, as it was a better version of the M-16 for jungle fighting – a weapon modified to the M4-A1 that has been a steadfast weapon of U.S. spec ops and soldiers for more than 20 years.

And, in SOG Chronicles Volume One, there's a story of SOG's hidden resource – the top secret supply chain that provided the CAR-15s, indigenous rations, rucksacks and rigged enemy ammo dubbed "Eldest Son" and the man who oversaw that supply network, Conrad Bennet "Ben" Baker.

Last, but not least, in future books we will produce stories about SOG teams that went missing in action during the secret war and remain posted by the U.S. government today as missing in Southeast Asia. At this writing in August 9, 2017, there were still 50 Green Berets listed as MIA in Laos alone, along with approximately 250 aviators and crew members, of which, at least 105 died supporting SOG teams in Laos. They are among the 1,606 Americans, both civilians and military service members who remain listed as missing in action.

In the fall, SOG Chronicles will begin interviewing soldiers for Volume Two of SOG Chronicles, with an eye toward going to press by the summer of 2018.

I close noting the dark, unforgiving, ruinous side of the Internet. Earlier this year, a government official told me he received a phone call from a "young writer" from an online news service with an opening line and question: "I'm working on a story about the 1998 use of sarin gas in Laos, I believe the black op was called Operation

Tailwind. Do you know how many American dissidents died from that attack?"

That government official was stunned: "I couldn't believe it, 47 years later a writer was looking to make a name for himself, as CNN and Time had done in 1998." He couldn't believe the erroneous story had surfaced again. As McCarley said during a 2015 interview, "Those lies keep coming back to haunt us, so we just have to deal with one lie at a time and if they print it, we'll sue 'em."

Here's a link to CNN's Tailwind story retraction:
http://edition.cnn.com/US/9807/02/tailwind.johnson/index.html

Here's a link to the complete text of First Amendment Attorney Floyd Abrams' report on his independent investigation of CNN's broadcast "Valley of Death:"
http://edition.cnn.com/US/9807/02/tailwind.findings/index.html

Below is a link to the Time magazine retraction, but the news magazine posted its June 15, 1998 original story with the headline: "Did The U.S. Drop Nerve Gas?"

The Subheadline read: "A CNN investigation charges that the U.S. used gas in 1970 to save roops sent into Laos to kill defectors." Then it printed this editorial note:

Retraction Appended: July 13, 1998

After the publication of this article and the broadcast of a CNN program on NewsStand: CNN & TIME provoked strong denials, both news organizations launched their own separate investigations. Each concluded that the allegations that sarin nerve gas was used by U.S. forces in a secret operation in Laos, known as Tailwind, and that U.S. defectors were intentionally killed were not supported by the evidence. You can read the full apology note in TIME here.

However, in order to read the "full apology" anyone who doesn't subscribe to Time magazine has to click on the word "here" and then pay a subscription to read it!

http://content.time.com/time/magazine/article/0,9171,988536,00.html

On the CNN website, on July 2, 1998, then, Time Managing Editor Water Issacson's statement on CNN's Tailwind coverage appeared:

July 2, 1998
Web posted at: 2:29 p.m. EDT (1429 GMT)

Like CNN, Time is retracting the story and apologizing for running it. Based on our own investigation and that conducted by CNN, we have concluded that the facts simply do not support the allegations that were made. A piece saying so will be in Monday's issue. We respect the serious and forthright way that CNN has re-examined this story, and we look forward to continuing to collaborate with them. We have learned a lot from the mistakes made, and we will try to avoid them in the future.

FINAL NOTE: There were law suits and settlements with some of the men involved with Tailwind, all of which were sealed. In 2005, a liberal judge threw out a case where Houston Attorney James Moriarty was representing three SF men who appeared in the CNN newscast. The judge essentially said that because the trio was in the military at the time they were slandered, they were technically a part of the U.S. Government, and thus the media could say anything about them without recriminations. Moriarty added, "CNN depicted the soldiers on Operation Tailwind as war criminals," and that "for each allegation, CNN selectively edited information to deliberately cause a misleading impression." He added that when the network faced the court of public opinion in the wake of the Tailwind programs, they were found guilty of poor, even prejudiced, journalism. "CNN lied in its broadcast about these men and their brave mission," he concluded.

GLOSSARY

AA – Antiaircraft.

AAA – Antiaircraft artillery.

ABCCC – Airborne Command and Control Center. Code names: Hillsborough, Moon Beam, Alleycat, Batcat. They were Air Force aircraft that were airborne 24/7 over Southeast Asia.

After Action Report (AAR) – After a recon team or hatchet force returned from a mission, team members were interviewed by intelligence officers while the team leaders would write a detailed report on the mission, which included such minutiae as vegetation coloration, height of triple-canopy jungle and soil composition.

A-1 Skyraider – Code names: Sandy, Spads, or Hobos. A Douglas-manufactured propeller-driven, single-reciprocal engine, land or carrier-based aircraft capable of carrying heavy bomb loads with long loiter time over targets. Loved by SOG teams, dreaded by enemy troops.

Arc Light – Code name for B-52 strikes. Arc Lights were devastating because no one could hear the B-52s flying overhead. Only when the ordnance began exploding on enemy targets did people know they were under attack.

Article 15 – Under the Military Code of Uniform Justice, a soldier could be fined and have his rank reduced for Article 15 infractions.

Area of Operations (AO) – Four primary target areas for SOG teams: Laos first code-named Shining Brass, then Prairie Fire; Cambodia – Daniel Boone, then Salem House; North Vietnam – Nickle Steel, and the DMZ.

ARVN – Army of the Republic of (South) Vietnam.

Army Signal Agency/National Security Agency (ASA/NSA) – U.S. intelligence organizations that intercepted enemy radio transmissions, broadcasts with highly specialized trained linguists, some of whom worked at SOG radio relay sites and with SF A Teams. ASA had a camp at Phu Bai on the west side of Highway 1, near the Hue/Phu Bai Airport.

AK-47 – Soviet manufactured 7.62 mm assault rifle used by NVA forces, Pathet Lao, Khmer Rouge and Chinese advisors. It became the standard infantry weapon used by Communist Bloc nations by the end of the 60s. Highly reliable with a distinctive bark from American CAR-15s or M-16s.

Authentication – A procedure used to confirm an individual's identity while talking with rescue forces on a survival radio.

Beeper – A radio transmitter that also emits a distinctive, high-pitch, wavering audible tone used as a homing device when tracked by a radio compass. All U.S. and Vietnamese team leaders on Recon Teams and Hatchet Forces carried the URC-10 emergency radio that had the beeper transmitter. It could be used for voice transmissions, especially when the communists jammed the FM channels used by teams on the ground.

Billets – Common term for military housing.

Bingo – Word used when Covey passed over Recon Teams or Hatchet Forces in the AO to help pinpoint location of team in the jungle.

Bomb Damage Assessment (BDA) – Reconnaissance of targets after B-52 strikes hit them – first thought to be an easy assignment, however, the reality of being on the ground proved that BDAs usually turned into fierce fire fights with enemy troops.

Blackbirds – Black-painted U.S. Air Force C-130 and C-123 medium cargo aircraft used to transport SOG teams and for other top secret transport and resupply missions in Southeast Asia and elsewhere.

Bright Light – SOG code name for heavily-armed Recon Teams inserted behind enemy lines to rescue downed pilots, recon team members escaping and evading the enemy or to locate and retrieve U.S. personnel killed in action, or to obtain proof of their death.

Browning Hi-Power – A 9 mm pistol carried by some SOG members due to large magazine capacity.

BRU – Many Montagnard tribesmen were recruited for SOG recon teams and hatchet forces. The Bru were considered to be among the lowest on the Montagnard social ladder; however, once trained by SF personnel, they proved to be excellent combat troops.

Caribou – An Army, two-engine cargo plane that was capable of flying at slow speeds and thus capable of landing and taking off on short runways in denied or contested areas.

CAR-15 – The Colt submachine gun, the preferred weapon of choice among SOG Recon Team and Hatchet Force men. It had a shorter barrel than the M-16, a collapsible stock and a limited flash suppressor.

CBU – Cluster bomb unit. Air Force ordnance dropped on enemy targets. The ordnance would have canisters packed with hundreds of small, explosive packets that would detonate when they hit enemy troops or the ground, shooting out hundreds of fleshettes or darts. Not all rounds would explode. Those remaining on the ground would explode if enemy or friendly troops stepped on them. When dropped on enemy targets they sounded similar to a mini arc light.

Charlie – Nickname commonly used by U.S. personnel for the Viet Cong, the so-called local communists who fought in South Vietnam. The word was also used interchangeably referring to NVA troops, although the NVA troops were uniformed and generally better trained than VC troops. After the VC was devastated during the Tet Offensive of 1968, the VC/NVA propaganda arms portrayed the VC as indigenous troops, when in reality, the NVA commanded or dominated most VC units. The only people who believed the VC propagandists were the media.

Chief SOG – Official title of SOG commander.

CIB – Combat Infantryman Badge. Awarded to infantrymen after they engaged enemy forces in combat. The CIB was established during WW II to honor Army infantrymen.

Claymore Mine – A deadly, plastic anti-personnel mine that contained 700 steel ball bearings that were fired by 1.5 pounds of plastic explosive that could wreak havoc up to 250 meters. It could be detonated by firing cord or time fuse that sent out a swath of ball bearings that could cut down small trees.

Commanding Officer (CO) – The ranking officer in charge at a military base or operation.

Command and Control Detachment (C&C) – The field headquarters in Da Nang for SOG missions into Laos, DMZ and North Vietnam.

Command and Control Central (CCC) – SOG base in Kontum, South Vietnam. Also called FOB 2.

Command and Control North (CCN) – SOG base north of Marble Mountain in Da Nang. Originally called FOB 4, before becoming CCN when FOB 1 teams were reassigned to Da Nang in 1969.

Command and Control South (CCS) – SOG base at Ban Me Thuot that ran mostly Cambodian and in-country targets. CCS combined the manpower of FOB 5 and FOB 6 in 1969.

Concertina Wire – A coiled type of barbed wire used in defensive positions.

Covey – Call sign for U.S. Air Force Forward Air Controllers for SOG. They flew in two-engine O-2 Cessna Skymasters until late 1969 when the OV-10 Bronco entered the AO.

Covey Rider – Experienced, cool-under-pressure Special Forces veteran recon men who flew with Covey to better relate with teams on the ground during SOG missions across the fence and to assist in directing air strikes.

Cravat – A large triangular bandage that doubled as a head bandana for many SOG troops because they made no noise in the jungle.

Daniel Boone – Code name for Cambodia AO. In early days of SOG, called Salem House.

Demilitarized Zone (DMZ) – 17th parallel dividing North and South Vietnam.

Det Cord – Abbreviation for detonation cord. An explosive cord use to detonate ordnance or to clear LZs of small trees.

Distinguished Service Cross (DSC) – Second highest Army valor award, second only to the Medal of Honor.

Drop Zone (DZ) – A landing area for parachutists or supplies dropped from an aircraft rigged to parachutes.

Dry Holes – A target where the SOG team had no contact with the enemy during the mission.

Executive Officer (XO) – the second in command at a military base.

5th Special Forces Group (Airborne) – Official headquarters in Nha Trang for Green Berets assigned to Vietnam. SOG personnel were recruited from the 5th Grp. for the top-secret missions.

1st Special Forces Group (Airborne) – Okinawa-based Green Berets assigned to SOG missions and Forward Observations Base for six months of temporary duty before 5th Group volunteers assumed SOG missions.

Flash – A colored cloth SF group designator sewn on green berets.

Flashy – A nickname for signal mirrors.

FNU – First name unknown.

Fucking New Guy (FNG) – An insulting reference to new men in camp.

Forward Operating Base (FOB) – SOG operations bases that reported to CCN, CCC & CCS: Ho Nunc Tao, FOB 6; Ba Me Thuot, FOB 5; Da Nang, FOB 4; Khe Sanh, FOB 3; Kontum, FOB 2 and Phu Bai FOB 1. After Khe Sanh was closed in June 1968, Mai Loc was called FOB 3 for several months before it was shut down. In the early SOG years FOB 1 was in Kham Duc. In early days of SOG most of the FOBs reported to C&C Detachment in Da Nang. C&C was moved to FOB 4, in '68.

Green Bombers – A nickname for stimulant pills designed to keep people awake.

Green Hornets – Code name for U.S. Air Force's 20th Special Operations Squadron which flew SOG missions into Cambodia without TAC Air cover from fast-movers and A1 Skyraiders.

Grease Gun – An older 9 mm submachine gun replaced by the CAR-15 on most SOG Recon Teams and Hatchet Force elements.

Grenade Launcher – The M-79 is a single-shot, break-open, breech-loaded shoulder weapon that fires 40mm projectiles and weighs approximately 6.5 pounds when loaded. A good grenadier could fire five to seven well-aimed rounds in a minute. Most Recon Teams and Hatchet Force companies predominantly carried high explosive rounds. Other ordnance available included buckshot, tear gas, white phosphorous, fleshettes or smoke.

Gunship – A combat helicopter that could be armed with a variety of M-60 machine guns that fired 7.62 mm rounds, 12.7 rockets, automatic 40 mm grenade launchers, mini-guns that could fire 6,000 7.62 mm rounds a minutes. In addition, the UH-1C (Huey) had to doorgunners, each armed with M-60 machine guns.

Hatchet Force (HF) – Code name for SOG operational platoons and companies. A platoon-sized force of approximately 35-40 men, including five or six Green Berets as squad and platoon leaders.

Hickory – SOG radio relay site for reconnaissance teams in Laos and North Vietnam. ASA/NSA personnel also ran radio intercepts from the site northeast of FOB 3 at Khe Sanh.

Head Shed – A nickname for headquarters staff office.

High Explosive, HE – A type of anti-personnel artillery, mortar, rocket and grenade ordnance designed to kill enemy forces with explosive shrapnel.

High Standard HD – A .22 caliber, silenced pistol SOG members carried for assassinations or silent kills on trails.

Ho Chi Minh Trail Complex – A series of supply trails that ran from North Vietnam, into Laos, through the Tri-Border Area and into Cambodia, established by the NVA. The North Vietnamese government established the 559th Transportation Group to move supplies down the trail. The group is so named because that was when the orders were signed officially establishing it after communists had begun moving south a year earlier. Its sole mission was to expand the trail and keep out SOG troops. A series of small trails branched off of the trail into South Vietnam, with the A Shau Valley as a major intersection. Many portions of the trail could not be observed from the air because the routes were camouflaged under jungle canopy.

Immediate Action Drill (IA Drill) – Practiced maneuvers for recon teams to break contact with the enemy.

Indig – An abbreviation of the word indigenous, as in indigenous SOG troops, pronounced (in-didge).

Jolly Green Giant – When no other aircraft could rescue recon teams during an extraction, the Sikorsky HH-3E helicopters were called because they were heavily armored and carried more firepower than conventional Army and Marine troop-carrying choppers. Later upgraded to CH-53.

Jump Wings – The U.S. parachutist's badge awarded upon completion of airborne training, which includes making five parachute jumps. Most soldiers had to obtain their jump wings prior to applying for acceptance in the U.S. Special Forces Qualification Training course at Ft. Bragg, N.C.

KIA – Killed in action.

Kilometer – 1,000 meters or 0.62 miles. The abbreviated term is Klick.

Kingbee – The code name for the South Vietnamese Air Force 219th Special Operations Squadron-flown helicopters that supported SOG missions. South Vietnamese pilots and crews manned the Sikorsky nine-cylinder H-34s helicopters. Most SOG teams preferred extraction by Kingbee because the ship could take more hits from enemy gunfire than the lighter Bell model helicopters.

KKK – Cambodian mercenaries assigned to SOG Hatchet Force platoons and companies. They wore distinctive red scarfs.

LLDB – Luc Luong Dac Biet (South Vietnamese Special Forces).

Landing Zone, LZ – A clear area of jungle large enough for a helicopter to land and deposit or pick up SOG troops.

Leghorn – SOG radio relay and NSA/ASA signal intercept site in Laos.

Little People – A term of endearment by SF troops for their indigenous personnel.

LRP or LRRP – Long-Range Reconnaissance Patrol rations, pronounced: LURP. LRRPs were dehydrated; men only had to add water to the plastic bag, wrap it up, place the bag against their stomach while the food absorbed the water and body heat.

M-16 – Fully automatic, air-cooled assault rifle that fired a 556 mm round either fully automatic or semi-automatic. It is the weapon most associated with conventional forces during the Vietnam War.

M-26 – Older U.S. produced fragmentation grenade.

M-33 – Newer, "baseball" grenade.

M-60 – 7.62 mm machine gun occasionally carried for additional firepower.

M-72 – Light Anti-Tank Weapon (LAW), 66 mm, disposable, single-shot anti-tank rocket launcher.

M-79 – Many SOG spike teams carried sawed-off N-79 grenade launchers that fired a 40 mm high-explosive round.

Machine Guns – Weapons where the bullets are fed into it by a belt or linked rounds and can be fired on full automatic until the machine gunner either runs out of bullets or the weapon overheats. The three predominant machine guns during the Vietnam War were the M-2 50-caliber heavy machine gun, the M-1919A6 30-caliber and M-60 7.62 mm machine gun that replaced the heavier 30-caliber weapon.

Medevac – Medical evacuation helicopter. In SOG they were called Chase Ships, where an SF medic would be aboard an extra helicopter in the event one of the troop-carrying helicopters got shot down.

MIA – Missing in action.

McGuire Rig – A harness at the end of 150-foot ropes dropped into jungle to pick up SOG personnel from heavily wooded areas that had no clear spots for a helicopter to land for a team extraction.

Military Assistance Command Vietnam – Studies and Observations Group (SOG) – A joint-service high command for unconventional warfare engaged in classified operations throughout Southeast Asia. The 5th Special Forces Group shipped personnel to SOG through Special Operations Augmentations (SOA) that provided the cover name given to the secret war conducted from 1964 through 1972 where billions of operational dollars were hidden in Navy and CIA budgets.

Montagnards – Hill tribesmen and social outcasts from South Vietnam who were fearless fighters recruited by SF for A Camps and SOG units. SF affectionately called them 'Yards.'

Mortars – There were three smooth-bore, muzzle-loaded, single-shot, high angle of fire mortar tubes used by U.S. forces during the war that varied from the smaller M-19 60 mm, to the M-29 81 mm and the heaviest of all, the M-30, 4.2 mortal that weighed more than 650 pounds when assembled and sat on a mortar plate.

Napalm – A jellied incendiary dropped from aircraft in large metal canisters that broke open upon contact with the ground or trees. The air and accelerants would then ignite the jellied substance into a huge ball of flame.

Nakhon Phanom Royal Thai Air Force Base (NKP) – SOG launch site, MLT-3, for operations into Laos and North Vietnam, especially when poor weather prevented teams from launching from South Vietnam into the AO.

NCO – Non-commissioned officer. Any soldier with the rank of E-4 through to E-9 Sgt. Major.

NCOIC – Non-commissioned officer in charge.

Nightingale Device – A diversionary device that was dropped onto an LZ. It was designed to sound like an ongoing firefight complete with gunfire and explosions, enabling SOG teams to safely insert into another LZ.

Nungs – Highly respected tribesmen and warriors of Chinese origin employed by several SF groups and SOG.

OIC – Officer in charge.

One-One – Code name of SF SOG Recon Team assistant team leader.

One-Two – Code name of SF SOG Recon Team radio operator, usually the latest member to join team.

One-Zero – Code name of SF SOG Recon Team leader. Position based on experience, generally. One-Zeroes had final say on teams, including rejecting officers and senior NCOs as potential team members.

OSS (Office of Strategic Services) – During World War II the OSS ran many secret operations in Europe and Southeast Asia. Several OSS operators went on to serve in clandestine operations in Korea during the Korean War. Some would rise to the position of Chief SOG during the Vietnam War. The OSS proceeded the CIA.

Panels – Bright-colored panels of various sizes that teams used as markers for aircraft.

PDQ – Pretty damned quick. As in, "Get here PDQ or we're dead."

Pen Flares – A small, single-round flare that was fired from a hand-held launcher, used to get the attention of friendly aircraft in the area. Sometimes it would be confused with enemy tracers.

Prairie Fire – Code name for SOG area of operations in Laos. Earlier code name for Laos was Shining Brass.

Prairie Fire Emergency – An emergency alert for recon teams in Laos. It signaled that a team was in contact with enemy forces and could not continue a mission – and probably was fighting for its life. Once a One-Zero declared a PFE, all air assets within range were diverted to assist the team, including Air Force, Marines Corps and Navy.

Project Delta – SF unit designed to operate in South Vietnam but was occasionally called to assist SOG teams or hatchet forces that were engaged in heavy combat with the enemy.

Project Eldest Son – Mortar rounds or rifle-propelled grenades that SOG had rigged to explode when used by NVA troops. SOG teams inserted Eldest Son ammo in enemy ammo caches, or along enemy trails. When used by enemy troops, it would explode, wounding or killing all personnel near the tampered ordnance.

Quang Tri – Launch site for FOB 1 and later CCN teams going to PF AO or DMZ.

Rear Echelon Mother F***** (REMF) – Personnel who stayed behind in base camps and often hassled troops going to the field. Generally despised by operational troops.

Republic of (South) Vietnam, RVN – U.S. ally.

Remain Over Night (RON) – Code name for site where team spends the night in AO.

Radio Direction Finding (RDF) – NVA and Russian personnel had strong radio-direction-finding equipment where they could triangulate between two listening posts and a team on the ground to ascertain the team's location.
RPD – A quality communist machine gun that fired a 7.62 mm round.
Rocket Propelled Grenade (RPG) – Used by NVA and VC elements.
Round-eye – An expression connoting American troops.
Rucksack – A type of backpack used in SOG, which always seemed uncomfortable and ill-fitting. It was specifically designed for the indigenous troops, smaller than conventional backpacks.
S-1 – Personnel staff on base and at FOBs.
S-2 – Intelligence staff on base and at FOBs.
S-3 – Operations staff, men who planned missions.
S-4 – Supply staff.
SAM – Surface-to-air missiles.
Scarface – Radio call sign of Marine gunships assigned to SOG from HMLA 367 Squadron. This squadron is still on active duty in Hawaii.
Shining Brass – Code name for Laos area of operation until 1967 when changed to Prairie Fire.
Sigma and Omega Projects – Early SOG projects for Daniel Boone and Tri-Border AO later absorbed into CCS.
Sihanoukville – Cambodian seaport where communist bloc nations shipped tons of supplies to NVA troops who trained in and launched military operations from Cambodia. By 1970 the NVA had 100,000 combat troops in 'neutral' Cambodia.
Situation Report (SITREP) – Radio reports from teams on the ground explaining their situation during the mission.
Slicks – A nickname for UH-1 series of troop, transport helicopters designed by Bell that replaced the Sikorsky H-34 in Regular Army units. Also called Hueys, in lieu of UH-1.
SKS – Early rifle used by NVA and Viet Cong forces.
Smoke – SOG teams carried smoke grenades to assist in directing air strikes, with varied colors from violet to white.

Soap Chips – A version of Eldest Son, where AK-47 ammo was tampered with to explode when used by enemy troops. Most SOG teams carried it and dropped it in the AO or enemy weapons/ammo caches.

SOP – Standard Operating Procedure, a common phrase in military meaning there is a standard procedure or way to do something, which is not always a good thing.

Spectre – Heavily armed Air Force C-130 transport aircraft with computerized weapons systems that linked to ground troops by locking in on the team's strobe light. They were preceded by Spooky – a C-47 gunship, then Shadow and Stingers – both of which carried computerized weapons systems aboard C-119 aircraft. Spectres remain a permanent component of the Air Force's Close Air Support today around the world.

Special Forces (SF) – The official military term for Green Berets, men who completed the Special Forces Qualification Course, earning the right to wear the distinctive headgear awarded to America's unconventional soldiers.

Spike Team – Code name for SOG recon team. At FOB 1 in '68, Spike Team was common phraseology for recon teams. By '69, Recon Team became the common term and designator among SOG personnel.

Sterile – All SOG personnel and weapons were unmarked and untraceable, for plausible deniability if captured by enemy troops on missions across the fence into Laos, Cambodia or N. Vietnam.

Strap-hanger – The term for someone who is assigned to a recon team at the last minute to run a mission. Usually not a member of that team, but used to fill out the number of U.S. personnel on a team. Could be from another team, who runs only one mission with another team.

Strobe Light – A small but bright, blinking light carried by SOG teams. Air Force gun ships in '68 deployed aircraft that could link to the strobe light, and direct ordnance against any enemy targets surrounding the team.

Strings – A term for ropes hung from helicopters to extract SOG troops from the jungle with no LZs. First strings were 150-ft. ropes, with sandbags attached to the ends to carry the rope to the jungle floor. Team members wore only a rope Swiss seat, which entwined around legs and waist. Later, a McGuire rig was attached to the rope for extractions. STABO rig was designed as a part of SOG teams' web gear for safer extractions.

Sten Gun – The WW II Sten Mk IIS submachine gun replaced by CAR-15.

Swedish K – A 9 mm submachine gun, popular in early SOG years, replaced by CAR-15

Syrette – A small syringe, that had a metallic tube containing morphine, with a needle attached to the end, complete with a plunger to open the flow of the needle, all contained in a clear, plastic tube. Every team carried at least one packet of morphine syrettes to the field.

TAC Air – An abbreviation for tactical air power. When a recon team used TAC Air, it would usually mean fixed-wing aircraft, such as F-4 Phantom jets, or A1-H Skyraiders.

The Peoples Army of North Vietnam (NVA) – The North Vietnamese Army uniformed personnel from communist-controlled North Vietnam who began moving south in force in 1959 to boost the VC – a fact little reported in the early years of the war.

TOC – Tactical operations center.

Toe-popper – The M-14 anti-personnel mine that was large enough to blow off a person's toes upon detonation. SOG teams left them in their trail to slow down NVA trackers.

URC-10 – Ultra-high frequency emergency radio/emergency beeper all SF carried.

UZI – Israeli-manufactured submachine gun used by some SOG teams. UZI had 9 mm and .45 caliber models.

'Yard – American slang for Montagnard tribesman.

Viet Cong, (VC) – Indigenous South Vietnamese communists. Only operated in South Vietnam.

Visual Reconnaissance (VR) – Fly over of target area to pick LZs before SOG missions across the fence.

White Phosphorous, Willie Pete, or WP – A type of explosive ordnance used in artillery, mortars, rockets or grenades. When the rounds exploded, they emitted white smoke and a deadly spray of white phosphorous – which, when it contacted human skin would continue to burn until it burned out or was suffocated by mud. Sometimes during mortal combat with the NVA, some recon teams tied a WP to a claymore mine, enhancing its deadly kill power.

WIA – Wounded in action.

Zero-One – Indigenous counterpart on spike team to One-Zero. On ST Idaho Nguyen Van Sau had run SOG missions for several years by '68.

Zero-Two – SOG spike team interpreter. On ST Idaho Nguyen Cong Hiep had run SOG missions for several years by '68.

Zero-Nine – SOG spike team M-79 team member, who also carried a Colt .45 Model 1911A pistol.

ABOUT THE AUTHOR

Born 19 January 1946, John Stryker Meyer entered the Army on 1 December 1966, completed basic training, advanced infantry training, jump school and graduated from the Special Forces Qualification Course in December 1967. After a 12-week training session in Ft. Gordon, on radio teletype, Meyer landed in South Vietnam in April 1968, and arrived at FOB 1 in Phu Bai in May 1968, where he joined Spike Team Idaho. When FOB 1 was closed in January 1969, ST Idaho was helicoptered to FOB 4 in Da Nang, Command and Control North, CCN. He remained on ST Idaho through the end of his tour of duty in late April. In October 1969 he rejoined ST Idaho at CCN. That tour of duty ended suddenly in April 1970. Meyer served as president of the Special Operations Assoc. from 2011-2014, currently works at the non-profit Veterans Affordable Housing Program, based in Orange, Ca, is a freelance writer for SOFREP.com, and serves as co-chairman of the One VA Community Advocacy Board. He is a trustee for the Veterans Associations of North (San Diego) County, a life member of the SOA, and holds membership credentials in the Special Forces Association, VFW, Military Order of The Purple Heart, American Legion, and the US Army Psychological Operations Veterans Assoc. He and his wife Anna have five children. They live in Oceanside, Ca.

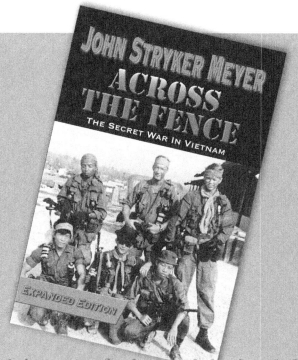

Printed in Great Britain
by Amazon

56487003R00119